The Promise

A Story of Faith, Love, and Forgiveness

By

John Stone

JohnStoneBooks.com

Dedication

This is dedicated to all of my family and friends that have stood by me through the most difficult trials and tribulations of my life.

This is also dedicated to my son, Jonathan. Jonathan, I am so proud of you for having the strength to endure all of life's difficulties, and to be able to not only survive, but also thrive. I will love you forever. I can't wait to see all the magnificent plans that God has for your life. As I have always told you, you are truly destined for greatness.

This is dedicated to everyone that needs hope in their lives. Everyone that needs a miracle. And everyone that needs the promises of God fulfilled in their lives.

Finally, this is dedicated to God. The God that Promised me the impossible, and then did it. The God that moved the heavens and the earth to make a way for my son. Thank you, Father, for bringing my son home. I will tell the whole world of Your greatness.

Table of Contents

Chapter One
The Promise

The final chapter has been written. The joyful ending I've only dared to dream of has arrived. I ask myself, am I dreaming, or has my dream become a reality? It's like I've just been awarded the largest lottery jackpot in the history of the world.

My hopes, my dreams, and everything that I have believed in has finally come to pass. At the beginning of this journey, in my innermost being, I knew I would write this book. But who could possibly believe my story? It was an outrageous thought. It has stirred up some very painful emotions, but as I look back, I can see the presence of God in our lives. I have to put this in writing. I want to testify of the incredible ways God has answered my prayers. I must let others know there is a hope that doesn't disappoint.

This is the account of God's divine intervention when everyone else told me it was impossible. It is the chronicle of what my son and I lived through and triumphed over.

Let me share with you how it all began...

I never believed in the romantic version of the "Love at first sight" concept. I never thought such a thing could be real. I certainly never thought it could be applicable to a soul other than a significant other. I never really believed in it until it happened. It was on December 2, 2002, when I experienced the greatest joy that a man could experience on this earth. That joy, was the joy of becoming a father. It was from the very first moment that my eyes witnessed this precious miracle, that my heart was no longer mine, but would now forever belong to him.

The first time I was called dad, was in the operating room, where my fiancé Tiffany, had just given birth. It was kind of shocking. I had just become a father! I was in complete awe as this delightful little guy was placed in my arms. Tiffany was still being attended to because she had a C-section, so Jonathan was all mine to hold and hug. I was immersed in a love so strong I could hardly believe it. I thought love was for the real emotional types, but that isn't who I am. I'm a logical person. I love numbers. I like things to add up exactly as I expect them to.

I introduced myself to him. "Hi Jonathan, I am your dad and I'm always going to take good care of you. Have no fear my little one, I'll be right here to watch over you." It was breathtaking, just listening to my son's voice as I heard the sound of his first cries.

Jonathan and I had such a strong connection. I recognized that this precious little one that I held in my arms had a purpose. He had a specific assignment from God and I was going to be part of it! What an honor it was to be his dad!

Little did I know that our happy, comfortable, uncomplicated world was about to become a real-life horror story. In the beginning of this trial, the only thing I could be sure of was pain, gut-wrenching pain that never went away.

March 11, 2003 was when my son's mother and I ended our relationship. We were not married, just engaged. It was also the day she abducted my son. That day will always be carved on every cell and fiber of my being. I bear the scars to prove it. It was when my world fell apart, and my destiny had changed for all time. By the grace of God and His mighty promises, I was able to keep going. It was the hardest, most difficult road I've had to travel.

In the midst of my agony, God promised me that He would return my son to me. It was in March 2003 that God promised that He would someday bring my son Jonathan home and I would raise him. The promise God gave me helped keep me alive and with hope.

In this first chapter, I will take you with me as I walk down memory lane, and describe to you the story of the day my son was taken from me, and the sixty-six days and nights that would follow. It was the beginning of my very long and painful journey.

Let me take you on this journey with me for just a moment. While I experienced this portion of the journey for sixty-six days, and sixty-six nights, I ask that you join me, and experience this portion of the journey for yourself, but for only a fraction of the time. In the following several pages, I will describe to you the heartbreaking experience I had during the time that my infant son was taken from me. I will describe my experience to you, not from my perspective, but from a perspective that you can immerse yourself into. Think of it as virtual reality. You can step into my shoes for a moment, and feel what I felt, during this difficult and trying time in my life. This is how the journey begins:

Missing

Child

Have you seen this child? He has been abducted from his father and was last seen at the Town Center Mall on March 11, 2003. If you know the whereabouts of this child, please contact the police or his dad. No detail is too small or insignificant. He is desperately loved and missed!

On March 11, 2003, for no reason at all, my life was taken from me. All I could do was watch as my world came crashing down. While the world crumbled around me, I reached up from underneath the ruins, trying to hold on to the hope that God had given me. It was because of the promise that the Lord gave me that I would rise each morning and continue to push past the insufferable pain of losing my son.

Now this is where I ask you to immerse yourself into the experience and feel all the emotions for yourself...

Close your eyes and imagine. Each morning as you rise, as tears fall from your eyes, you look, and all you see is emptiness all around. Your heart aches from the sword that has pierced your soul. There is nothing that can ease the pain. You search for hope, and the only thing you find is agony. Worse still, you realize that nothing can prepare you for what is still to come.

Close your eyes and imagine. Imagine your desperation. Imagine the frustration. Imagine, that it is only when you close your eyes, that you once again can see your child.

As time passes, the smiles and cries of this beautiful baby become more and more distant and are no longer part of your daily life. You realize that you will never be able replace all that was taken from you. Nor will you be able to close your eyes and recall your son as he was at four months, five months, or six months of age. The only thing you can do, is close your eyes and imagine.

As you begin to imagine the sound of his first word as it came out of his mouth, you remember the sound of his voice as he cried, and that sound echoes in your mind, at a volume that is so intense, that the sound of it shatters your soul.

Close your eyes and imagine. Imagine that as you awaken every morning, you do your best to ignore the pain. You try to push through the day, doing all you can to ignore the torment that is racing through your mind. All day long, you try not to think about your child. Your wish is to simply make it through the day. Your efforts are worthless, because each time you hear the sound of a baby crying, it brings tears to your eyes. You see a stroller pass by, and your heart skips a beat, as it reminds you of your precious child. Your wish is for nothing more than to be able to hold him in your arms once again. As time passes, this wish becomes nothing more than a dream that is fast fading.

Once again, I ask, that you close your eyes, and imagine. Imagine, that as you climb into bed, you attempt to rest your mind, body, and soul, but the anguish once again begins to consume you. You are tormented as thoughts of your child race through your mind. All night, you toss and turn without a single moment of sleep. All this, before you must rise again, to face it all over again. Imagine that you do this again and again, for sixty-six days and sixty-six nights.

One last time, I ask, that you close your eyes and imagine. Imagine that this is your child

This is how the greatest testimony of my life begins. This struggle will be used by God to show me His greatness and His strength, setting the stage for Him to work the most incredible miracle I have ever witnessed in my life. First, let me tell you how it began...

Chapter Two

In the Beginning

Florida nights in the winter are fantastic. By the time the sun sets, a refreshing cool breeze is blowing on you. The aroma in the air of the tropical fragrances reminds you that you are living in paradise. You can wake up to temperatures in the fifties, and then by early afternoon it will be in the mid to high seventies. I made the move from Massachusetts, two years earlier.

Prior to my move to Florida, I was a manager in a restaurant. The workplace in Florida was totally different. Management positions were hard to find, so I had to be content with my job as a cashier and cart attendant until a better position became available. I was not ashamed to do manual labor. I knew hard work and diligence would promote me. Besides, gathering carts in the parking lot kept me healthy and fit.

Later in life, I sat behind a desk for as many as eighty hours a week. I was a slave to my computer and always had a telephone between my ear and shoulders. My subsequent career choice of accounting would end up defining me, or at least a significant part of the way I saw myself for at least two decades.

During Christmas time the store I worked at required all employees to work after closing to clean up the mess that was made throughout the day. All the cashiers would be assigned to a different department each night to help straighten the merchandise. The store would close at eleven P.M., and we were required to work until one, sometimes two o'clock in the morning. I was working my tail off and Christmas time was especially chaotic. There was no Amazon or popular internet selling sites back then.

About a week before Christmas, I had the closing shift as a cashier. It was after eleven o'clock when the last customer left the store. On this night, I ended up in the detergent and pet supply aisles. I organized the merchandise on an end cap and another team member came over to work the same area. I didn't know her name, but I recalled seeing her work as a cashier earlier in the week.

She just started working at the store. Her name was Tiffany, and she was very cute. It was while we were working together that night that we introduced ourselves to each other. We started a conversation to make the time pass.

She told me she loved doing arts and crafts. The way she described her artistic talent was indeed intriguing. Tiffany's face lit up as she told me about her drawings. She loved inventive and creative projects. Tiffany's area of artistic expertise was paintings, sketches, and unique arts and crafts. Her subjects for paintings were people, animals and landscapes. I admired her multi-talented gifting. I told her that if I had anywhere near that talent, I would have sent my portfolio to Disney or some other huge company. I was lucky if I could draw a stick figure.

Numbers were always my thing. In elementary school, we would be called to the front of the class for a math problem on the board. I'd grab the piece of chalk and instantly write the answer. Many of my classmates would ask me, "How did you do that?" Most of the kids would struggle for several minutes trying to calculate the answer. I could always just look at a set of numbers and calculate the answer in my head in a nanosecond. Sometimes it would be a problem with my teachers because they required us to show how we came up with the answer. A lot of times I couldn't show how I arrived at the answer, I just knew in my head that it was correct. I'm sure I lost some points on my math assignments for not writing out things the way educators wanted, but honestly it was my God-given gift. I was a human calculator, and still am.

I shared with Tiffany that my talent was with numbers. That's what brought me to my seasonal job at H&R Block. I took the tax preparation course to earn some extra cash. I passed their test with a nearly perfect score of 98 and was hired. Up until that time Tiffany's taxes were done by her sister, Julie.

We shared a lot of our life experiences as we worked together at night. Some of Tiffany's stories were endearing, others were funny, still others caused me to want to know this attractive young woman more. In fact, I wanted to know everything about this girl, and it was just so nice to have a friend. We talked and worked until approximately one in the morning, but the hours flew by while I was working side by side with her.

A couple of weeks after our initial meeting, Tiffany brought me one of her pieces of artwork. It was my name written in calligraphy. I was blown away! Apparently, Tiffany was also thinking about me when I wasn't with her! She had signed and dated it and joked that it would be worth a lot of money someday when she was a famous artist.

As the weeks passed, I realized Tiffany had a major crush on me. I had business cards from my other job as a tax preparer and used it as the perfect excuse to get a date. I gave Tiffany one of them and told her to call me if she needed help preparing her taxes. She did call, and a few days later we went on our first date. I even had my car detailed for it!

I picked her up at her sister Julie's house. Our first date was a lot of fun. We went out to dinner and then just leisurely walked through a huge bookstore. Over the next several weeks, we continued dating and eating out regularly. Some of the places were upscale, others were diners and fast-food chains. Many times, after getting off at 1:00 AM or 2:00 AM, we would go and eat at the places that were open twenty-four hours a day. Often, we would go to the movies or take a walk on the beach. Sometimes, we went for two- or three-mile walks across the Big River Bridge.

Tiffany also loved to take me to the craft Store. This was her world. She loved introducing me to different venues of her artistic gifts. Paints, canvases and crafts got Tiffany so excited that she practically danced through the aisles. She delighted at the thought of creating something new and wonderful. Lots of times I just let her have as much time as she needed while I went next door to a Circuit City store. I was really enjoying our friendship. It was just terrific to have someone to share my ambitions and plans with. Looking back, I should have realized Tiffany was looking for a whole lot more than just a friend.

We finally got to the place where Tiffany wanted me to meet her whole family. At last it hit me, *Tiffany thinks our relationship is serious! Now what?*

Chapter Three
The Roller coaster Ride

Admittedly, after the first couple of days we spent together, I had a slight uneasiness. I couldn't determine what it was, but something inside of me was saying, *something is wrong, something is not quite right here. You need to slow down and find out why you are hesitating.* I had moved from Massachusetts and of course wanted to make new acquaintances, so I just pushed those uncomfortable feelings aside. Now I realize it was warning number one.

I pushed past the wisdom God was trying to give me. It caused me to make the biggest and most costly mistake of my life. I realize now that inner voice was the voice of the Lord, a kind and loving heavenly Father, trying to advise me, reaching out to me, and attempting to warn me. He was endeavoring to spare me from years of heartache. If only I had stopped to take some time to be alone with God. I needed to find out who was sounding all kinds of alarms and concerns, and what was He trying to get across to me?

After the first couple of dates, I thought I should tell her *let's just be friends*, but I argued, *she is cute and good company. I'm not dating anyone else right now so what's the harm? I don't have anything else to do, I might as well spend some time with her and see how it goes.*

I had recently graduated from a technical school. I had taken computer and electronics courses. I learned some basic computer repair skills that allowed me to start my own home-based business. I built and sold computers and repaired them too. I met some great people at the school, some of which became my friends, and some of them are still in my life today.

Most of the friends, however, noticed there was something very peculiar about this girl. Like me, they felt that something wasn't right. Several of them shared their concerns with me. It didn't take long for her behavior to become increasingly of concern to me and others as well. No one could quite put their finger on it, they just didn't feel I should continue with the relationship. The general consensus was that Tiffany was nothing but trouble. At that time, I couldn't understand how they could come to that conclusion when most of them only met her once or twice, but they saw how controlling she was. To me, Tiffany was mesmerizing. It was kind of like that Dr. Jekyll and Mr. Hyde thing. There were times when the chemistry and passion could be so strong and intense, and then there were times, that in an instant, she could turn into a raging maniac with no self-control over her fury.

My situation just changed so fast. Tiffany now started to demand all of my time and attention. I recall having mononucleosis early on in our relationship. I told her I couldn't see her one day because I was so sick and weak. I couldn't even get out of bed that one day. Tiffany was enraged. A normal person would have offered help and understanding. She was just livid, like I did something deliberate to cause it. She insisted that I just didn't care enough about her and didn't want to spend time with her.

The overbearing behavior started to increase. If I wanted to spend time with my friends, Tiffany would accuse me of cheating on her. It didn't take long before I wasn't allowed to have any friends, male or female. The domineering behavior intensified. Tiffany no longer wanted me seeing my own family. Although I still didn't see it, those closest to me began to see her as dangerous.

Brie was a friend I met at the technical school. Brie and I hung out together all the time. She was on a bowling league on Friday nights. We spent many casual Friday nights drinking Long Island ice teas and just relaxing. Brie and I were friends a little over a year when I met Tiffany. We spent so many fun times together, but that all ended when I met Tiffany.

I was young and didn't understand how to handle friendships with the opposite sex while being in a relationship.

I ended up choosing my romantic relationship with Tiffany over my friendship with Brie. I regret how many friends and people I abandoned. I now know what a mistake it was.

I had not seen or talked to Brie for many years, until my relationship with Tiffany ended. By then, Brie had gotten married, and became a stepmother to several young children. I first reconnected with her and her husband when they came to my office to have their taxes done. I know Brie was hurt by what I had done, and I hope she has forgiven me. She was one of the many people that told me, "That girl is crazy." But I didn't listen!

Another friend I dropped was my friend Daniel. He has been my best friend for so many years, even after I pushed him aside for two years. Tiffany was so controlling, so jealous that I wasn't allowed to have friends anymore. The sad part is, I allowed it. No one had a gun to my head. I think I saw Daniel maybe once during the two years I was with Tiffany. Daniel always had my back. When you have friends like that it's important to realize they are watching out for you, and if several of your closest friends and relatives are saying the same thing, heed what they are saying, it just might save your life!

Three weeks into my relationship with Tiffany, I went to the county fair with Brie and Daniel. We had gone the year before, and it was fun. It was hilarious to go to the fair with Daniel because he was scared of roller coasters and just about every ride there. We all went on the scrambler, a classic ride at the fair, and he literally screamed like a girl the whole ride. Brie and I cracked up laughing until we cried. It was one of those things you had to see. A grown man screaming like a little girl!

I had invited Tiffany to go with us, but she didn't want to. It was so early in our relationship that I hadn't seen how controlling, self-centered, and jealous she was. There was such a huge argument over it, it was the last time I saw either Daniel or Brie for a very long time. The contention lasted for several weeks. In her mind, I had cheated on her. Tiffany later used, "going to the fair with my friends" as a means of justifying cheating on me. There was a guy at work that had become interested in her and she would talk about him all the time. I have no doubt she went out with him while we were both dating. Tiffany never admitted it. Pathological liars rarely, if ever, tell the truth. When I asked her about it, she responded by saying, "Well you went out with Brie to the fair", as if to justify what she had done. If I were smarter back then, I would have let him have her!

Shortly after we started dating, I began working at H&R Block for my second tax season. I had just started my computer business, worked at the store where Tiffany and I met, and started a new job at a bank. I was up to my eyeballs in work. I'd leave the house at 7:00 AM, and go from one job to another job, and then to another job. After my long days at work, I would go visit Tiffany. Tiffany and I used to have a blast, going out to dinners, movies, romantic walks, etc.

For the first six months of my employment at the bank, they would send me up to Orlando one weekend a month for paid training. I was set up in really nice hotels like the Hyatt or Sheraton. We were two very young kids, experiencing brand new honors and privileges neither of us had ever been through. The Word of God clearly states, "There is pleasure in sin for a season". That was my season, but it quickly ended and became hell on earth.

I was living my dream because I was able to meet with many other new employees from the area. I looked forward to each new day's adventures and discoveries. We'd start our training early in the morning, then break for lunch, have an afternoon session, and then go back to the hotel to relax by the pool and use the gym. For a guy who was just starting out, having free meals, hotel stays, allowances for expenses, and reimbursement for mileage was really exciting. It felt so good to have the respect and perks of the corporate world. Tiffany would also come up as she was able.

There was one weekend in particular that stands out in my mind. After our morning training session one day, we broke for lunch, and I ended up having lunch with a lady named Rose. I will remember this woman as long as I live. It was like she was a messenger from God. Looking back, I now believe that God used her to try send me a message. However, I didn't listen.

One thing I do know, is that God has a plan for everything that happens in our lives. I don't believe things happen to us, I believe they happen for us. God can take any situation, no matter how dreadful it may appear to be, and turn it into our biggest successes, and our life's most defining moments.

Regardless, while Rose and I were having lunch, she asked me, with a very thick Spanish accent, about my girlfriend.

Because she was older than I was, and presumably had more life experience and wisdom than I did, I wanted to hear what she had to say. As it turned out, she was amazingly accurate in her assessment of my relationship with Tiffany.

As we talked, I told her about my girlfriend. I was excited to tell her about my new relationship, and how much I was really into this. I told Rose about how much fun Tiffany was, and how I looked forward to seeing her each day. However, Rose was able to see beyond my mask and feigned love. She was able to recognize things about Tiffany that I hadn't considered. She saw the warnings that God kept trying to tell me. While I spoke about Tiffany with excitement and enthusiasm, Rose identified characteristics about Tiffany that alarmed her. Rose warned me, telling me to be careful with Tiffany. She told me to end the relationship. She cautioned me if I stayed with this woman, she would ruin my life. Being so young and quite honestly naive, I didn't recognize the dangers she had seen. I saw Tiffany and our relationship as vibrant, fun, and energizing. I thought there could be a future for us. While there was a future relationship between us, it certainly was not the one I had imagined!

As spring passed, and summer rolled around, I started to make changes in my employment and also my personal life. My computer business continued to thrive and my job at the bank kept me very busy. What occupied my thought life most of all was my relationship with Tiffany. Our love had blossomed into a passionate romance, filled with highs and lows. I felt like I was on a roller coaster ride.

You get on the roller coaster, secure your safety belt, and take off. At the start, you race toward the sky, then there is the unexpected turn to the right, and then to the left. You're a mile high in the sky, then all of a sudden you drop. You are heading downward at a rate of speed that is uncontrollable. You are holding on for dear life.

You are not sure you are going to make it. You want to scream, but then you realize how humiliated you would be if anyone heard you! No one forced you to take this ride. You chose to.

As you finally come crashing down, the ride slows down, and you come to a stop. You look around, and as you slowly rise to your feet. You step out of the ride, and place your feet firmly on the platform, and you realize you survived, and you feel invincible.

You decide that you want to once again feel the excitement and adrenaline rush that you experienced while the rollercoaster was racing upwards towards the heavens. You realize that you want to be on top of the world again, looking out at the sweeping panoramic view of the world. So, what do you do? You get back in line, back on the roller coaster, and the ride takes you to some of the greatest heights you have ever experienced. Once again, you are filed with the rush of adrenaline and the sensation of excitement that keeps you coming back for more.

You have totally forgotten about what it was like to go over the top, and race downwards to what would appear to be the very end of life as you know it. Being so entertained by the ride as it goes up, you don't care that you know it's going to come speeding into a downward spiral and crash.

That is what my life was like. I was young, twenty-three, and extremely naive. I just wanted to know what it was like to be so alive, passionate and invincible. The only problem with that was the price I would ultimately have to pay.

Chapter Four

The Fire-Breathing Dragon

My job at the bank was also affected by my relationship with Tiffany. The company did a great job of promoting a team mentality. They planned company events and social gatherings for their employees. One such event was a canoeing trip scheduled in the summer of 2001. Needless to say, Tiffany did not want to go. Later, I realized it was because of her difficulty in interacting with others in a social environment. Tiffany's reluctance was also because of her monstrous jealousy and her controlling nature she displayed for all to see.

I wasn't allowed to look at, speak to, or even be in the presence of another female. If I so much as ran into a co-worker while we were out shopping, and that female co-worker simply said, "Hello", it would turn into a World War III battle of epic proportions.

As the relationship progressed, the jealousy grew. If we were walking through the mall, it was demanded of me that I keep my head down and look at the floor as we walked, in order to avoid accidentally glancing in the direction of another female. It had gotten so bad that one day as we were walking through the mall, I accidentally turned my head in the direction of a cardboard cutout of Britney Spears that was standing inside of an empty storefront window and literally, all hell broke loose. Tiffany accused me of staring at that piece of cardboard with such lustful desire, that she knew I wanted to engage in sexual relations with it. She was like a fire-breathing dragon with such toxic and cruel, sick demands. She saw every other woman as a rival, wanting to take 'her man'.

Over the two years we spent together, there was a never-ending barrage of fights over imagined evils of me with the opposite sex. Tiffany's constant and the daily fits of rage made it almost impossible to have a normal life at work and at home.

Tiffany lived in a world of continual crisis and chaos. If there wasn't a crisis going on, she would create the crisis. Tiffany simply could not live in a world of peace and calmness. I didn't find out the cause of her instability and her violent insanity until after our relationship ended.

I am not going into these details to discredit my former partner, but rather to warn other men and women. It is my desire that someone who is living in an abusive and toxic relationship, will be able to identify that they are in an unhealthy partnership. My hope is that they will get help or break off the relationship. If both people in a relationship are drowning, at least one of them has to leave or get help to survive, especially where there are children involved.

Going back to my time at the bank, my manager, Linda, sat me down to express her concerns over me never attending any of the team building events. Linda felt as though I was unwilling to be a "team player" and that it was affecting my other co-workers. She said she would like to see me improve that area of my work life with the bank. She also asked why I had chosen to snub my co-workers on a regular basis. I honestly don't remember what excuse I gave her, I'm sure I mumbled something about being overly busy with my computer business. I didn't have the nerve to tell her it was because my girlfriend wouldn't allow me to participate. It was easier to lie about my life than to have to face the fire-breathing dragon at home.

I was simply in survival mode. When you live in an environment that is constant chaos, you just survive. You keep evil secrets from your friends, (if you have any left) and you hide from your family the degradation and continual humiliation you are living with on a regular basis. You make up little "white lies" to cover up for the abuser. Keeping secrets about happy surprises or keeping a confidence for someone is a good thing. Having evil secrets to protect the guilty is not okay. I was living in shame and to share with another human being the hell I was in, would have been much too mortifyingly painful.

Looking back, I wonder what my life would have been like if I had chosen to end my relationship with Tiffany. There were many other bright and attractive women that I worked with that showed interest in me during my years at the bank. I realize that the difficulties I endured in my life could have been erased simply by making different choices in my past.

Have you ever stopped to consider what your present-day life would be like if you made a different choice about who you were dating, or where you lived, or worked? It's amazing to think that there could literally be hundreds and possibly thousands of different directions that your life could have taken, if you had done things differently.

Was everything that happened in my past a part of God's plan for my life? After all, with God being perfect in all His ways, how could my mistakes be part of His plan for my life? I thought it was His will for me and all of His children to live faith-filled, obedient lives and to serve, love, and trust Him. My early years were anything but pleasing to God.

God knew from the foundation of the world, what sins I would commit and what mistakes I would make. Because of His great love for me, He created a plan for my life, in spite of me. Like the GPS in your car, when you make a wrong turn, it immediately reconfigures a new way for you to get to your destination. You choose whether you will obey God's voice or not. I'm speaking from experience, life is much simpler when you choose God's way!

While I know that if I had chosen another woman to be the mother of my son, life for us would have been different, less painful and certainly not filled with such heavy burdens. I also realize that if I made a different choice, I would not have the same handsome, intelligent, and thoughtful, young man as my son. When I see how generous and caring he is, I realize that I am beyond blessed!

The circumstances upon which our lives were built, made each of us who we are today. It will also have a huge impact on who we will be tomorrow, and every day thereafter. Anyone who knows me well, will tell you I am one of the strongest, most resilient people they know. Would I be as strong if I had not gone through the fiery trials and tribulations that I was forced to endure?

Is the strength that I have acquired throughout the years a result of all that I have lived through? Will that strength be needed in the future to fight another battle that may have crushed a weaker man? Most importantly, would my son be the man he is, and would he be on track to be the man that God created him to be without all the adversities?

I don't think any of us could answer these questions, or even understand the purpose of all the heartache and suffering that we were forced to endure. It is my belief that the most important thing in this life is to trust Him. I trust in the God that carried us through all of these trials. God has allowed and equipped us in every heartache, false accusation, and horrible legal proceeding. I know God has allowed us to be more than conquerors. He gave us the power to endure.

I started writing this book in November 2016. During this time, the Lord prompted me to read in the Bible the book of Daniel about Shadrach, Meshach, and Abednego. They were three Hebrew teenagers that were thrown (literally) into a huge furnace. The men that threw them in were burned and killed while throwing them in. Even though the boys had winter garments on, the only thing that burned in the fire were the ropes that were tied around their wrists.

A fourth man appeared in the midst of the fire. It was Jesus. He not only gives us the power to stand, He also carries us through the fiery flames. The boys didn't even smell of smoke, although they were in the middle of flames, in a scalding furnace. I have faith that as you are going through a horrible situation, you also will not be burned in your sweltering trial. Jesus will carry you!

As the summer months continued, I kept getting on the roller coaster ride that we called a relationship. It was complete chaos at times, then at other times it was absolutely amazing. Over all we were never that compatible. We simply had that "chemistry". We had an unexplainable attraction.

Until this day, I can't understand how, or why we were so attracted to one another. I truly believe that it must have been the forces of darkness that pushed us towards each other. The devil himself tried to destroy my life, and capture my soul, by tempting me with a lustful, intense, and sinful lifestyle. I believe that Satan, as described in 1 Peter 5:8, spends his time scouring the earth searching for souls he can devour.

All of us are created by God and made in His image. However, only those who confess Jesus as the Lord of their lives, believe He died for their sins, rose again on the third day and ask Him to come into their hearts are actually God's children.

Because of Adam and Eve's sin they became Satan's children. Their blood became tainted, and all who came after them were born into sin. We were born into Satan's kingdom. When a person prays the simple prayer I've just spoken about, they switch kingdoms and join God's kingdom and become His children.

Satan saw that I was indeed one of God's most beloved children. At that time in my life, I was basically "on the fence" between the devil and God. I was primarily a law-abiding person, who tried to live a good life, but I never made the conscious decision to give my life to the Lord or to follow Him, and establish a relationship with God's Son, Jesus. He is the one who bridges the gap between God and His creation. Therefore, my soul was still up for grabs. Little did the devil know that God would take what he meant for my harm, and use it for my good, and for His glory, (Genesis 50:20). When Jesus was nailed to the cross, Satan thought he had won. He overplayed his hand. He thought he had destroyed humanity when he inspired the Pharisees to crucify Jesus.

When Jesus rose on the third day, hell was split wide open. Jesus took the keys of sin, sickness and the grave and gave them to His disciples. He gave whosoever would follow Him power to become the sons and daughters of God. Satan is limited. He uses deception, lies and temptations. Every one of us has the power to say, "No!"

The Wicked One goes on a path of destruction because he knows his time is limited, (Job 1:12) and he wants to take as many souls with him as possible before his time runs out. Now, I know it sounds as though I'm beginning to preach a lot here, and if this is not your thing, I understand. However, I beg you to please hang in there, as I believe that when you are finished reading this story, you also will be able to believe, or at least be led to take a long hard look at the possibility of accepting there is a force in this universe that is greater than we are.

Back to my life before God, after almost a year, and despite the arguing, and intense jealousy, I decided that love conquers all. I knew of Tiffany's controlling ways, her backbiting, violent and abusive behavior, yet I rationalized all of it. After all, even mentally ill people need love too, don't they? No one is perfect, I got this, is what I told myself.

With all the things I have shared with you, one would think that it can't get any worse. Trust me when I tell you that it did! The roller coaster ride continued, with our extreme ups and downs. I can't explain why I stayed so long, but hindsight is always twenty/twenty.

I'd like to take a moment now to share some of the fun times we had together, and some of the really crazy times.

Tiffany had always been a huge fan of music. She had collected hundreds and hundreds of CD's. About eight or ten months into our relationship, we decided to start a small business working as DJ's for weddings, birthday parties, and other events.

At the time, there was a gentleman named James Connor that wrote a weekly business column for the local newspaper. James had written a story on me a year before when I started my computer business. The article helped me gain a lot of attention in the community. It brought a lot of customers my way, and it kept me busy and making good money.

We got in contact with James again and he agreed to do a story about our new business. Mr. Connor came to my house to interview us and take photos for the business column he published. The pictures came out very well.

Our first job was a birthday party for a teenage girl. One young girl at the party asked us to play a Britney Spears song, and Tiffany became furious. She was smart enough to know not to start World War III in front of everyone. So, instead she moaned and groaned the whole night, making it miserable for me. When we got home, the rage and screaming started, and lasted all night and into the morning.

According to her relationship rules, as I mentioned earlier, I was not allowed to have any friends, male or female. I also wasn't even permitted to see my family, or to have conversations with female co-workers. I certainly couldn't listen to music performed by a female singer. Completely crazy, right? All the time, I was enabling her, allowing the insanity to keep on increasing.

All of these erratic behaviors, and controlling manipulative ways, were a result of Borderline Personality Disorder. In Tiffany's disturbed world, if you listened to a song with a female singer in it, it meant you were lustfully dreaming of having intense and passionate sex with the female singer. I am not exaggerating this. Tiffany's jealousy had no limits. Her need to control was never ending, and the chaos continued to increase.

No one wants arguing, contentious DJ's hosting their party. I knew Tiffany's rage and evil suspicions would only increase. I was trying to give the people that hired us a great event with a lot of energy and fun. After doing a couple more DJ parties, we decided it was not working, so we ended the business.

Chapter Five
Life in Fast Forward

Despite all the craziness and drama, I found myself in love with this woman. I don't know how it happened, it just did. Of course, the fact that we were sleeping together outside of marriage had formed a soul tie between us. That was why it was so hard for me to walk away. So, one night in January 2002, I decided to propose to her with a one karat diamond engagement ring. I will never forget the look of shear horror on my parent's faces when we told them of my plans. I know now they were sickened about the news because they foresaw the heartache ahead. During my relationship with Tiffany, not once had they verbally disapproved of my relationship with her, but I sensed a strong concern, heartache and anguish.

I wish they would have been more vocal, citing things that alarmed them. I'm not saying I would have listened. but it would have been worth a try. I know that kids, teens, and even young adults generally tend to not listen to the older and wiser. When we are young, we think we know it all. I thought I was invincible. I found out the hard way that I wasn't even close!

As the months passed, I was getting deeper and deeper into the tangled web Tiffany was weaving. I experienced the sensation like I was being smothered but I didn't understand why. I felt like I was in the web of a black widow spider while she was waiting to devour her prey. I never realized I was being manipulated. How could anyone be so naive? Despite being a mature, responsible, intelligent man, I surrendered to the chemistry, the lust, and the strong desire and yearning to be with someone.

All of this was the result of the absence of God in my life. If Jesus had been in my life, I would never have been so foolish as to desire the love and acceptance of someone who was so wrong for me.

Throughout the months following our engagement, Tiffany kept talking about how much she wanted a baby. I was in love, and willing to give her what she wanted. I wanted to make the person I loved happy. I thought if it was God's will and if it was meant to be, then it would happen. What a foolish way to think!

The truth is that God gives everyone a free will to choose. He doesn't make you choose whether to eat eggs or cereal each morning. He lets you choose. Because I wasn't seeking God's guidance for my life, all the choices and outcomes were of my choosing. I can't blame God for the heartache I brought upon myself. The wonderful part is that even when we totally blow it, God is merciful and kind. The minute we turn to Him, He will give us a plan and a way out of any mess we have created.

It was on April 17, 2002 that we found out we were having a baby. I was so excited, happy and nervous all at the same time. Never having had a child before, I was worried about whether I would know how to take care of a baby

Tiffany and I talked excitedly about how we would tell my parents that we were expecting a baby. I remember when my sister became pregnant with their son, my mom knitted a blanket for the baby as a gift. So, I decided to go to the store and purchase a couple rolls of yarn to bring to my mom when we told her. It was my attempt to soften the blow. Once again, as if in slow motion, I'll never forget the look on their faces, nor will I forget the deafening silence of both parents, sitting there with their mouths open, but no words coming out.

My mom was in her nightgown sitting in the recliner chair with rollers in her hair. My dad was sitting on the couch near her when we came in carrying a shopping bag. We awkwardly stood there and pulled the yarn out of the bag and handed it to my mother. While my mom said nothing, the look on her face spoke very loudly of shock, woundedness, and disbelief. After handing it to her we told her, "We are having a baby". I could also tell by the look on my dad's face that he was very upset, but he chose to keep his opposition to himself.

We went to Tiffany's sister, Rebecca's house next. The next stop after that was my brother's house. While we were at my brother's house, I called my sister in Illinois to share our good news. We continued to her sister Susan's house with our good news, then on to my sister's. Tiffany's sisters were all ecstatic, while my siblings responded with strained enthusiasm.

After letting everyone know of our sensational news, we went out having a blast shopping for baby stuff. Who knew a grown man could get so elated buying baby booties, diapers, toys and the like? It was so exciting to be young and in love. Having a baby just seemed like the next logical step on this never-ending journey of romance. It appeared to me that I was creating the life I always wanted.

Fortunately for us, there was a department store near us that was going out of business. We went there for our baby clothes, and things were discounted so much it was like they were giving the stuff away. We were lucky enough to be able to get everything we needed for next to nothing.

We didn't have a lot of money. Tiffany was working part time at a home improvement store, and I was working part time at the bank. I chose not to work at H&R Block during the 2002 tax season. Although I originally planned to work with them that season, the company and I could not agree on some of the terms of my contract, henceforth no work or extra money. Additionally, there was my computer business. The article I had in the newspaper brought me a lot of clients, but without money to continue a marketing campaign, the business slowly faded away.

Working in finances and management, I was naturally the type of person that would be concerned about the cost of caring for a child. I began to realize that my salary wasn't enough to provide the best things for my baby. After finding out we were having a baby, I went all over town filling out job applications, trying to get another job so I could make enough income to provide for my little one.

I continued to look for a good job with health benefits, but no other work came in. I did however, receive a call from a video store. The female manager left a voice mail on our answering machine. Tiffany heard the message and went into a violent tirade. "Who is this woman? Why is she calling you? You're sleeping with her, aren't you?"

In her own mind, Tiffany conjured up all types of evil imaginations, concerning me and other women. She went into another one of her violent tangents, screaming, throwing things, threatening me with physical violence and all the other chaos that comes along with Borderline Personality Disorder. I wasn't allowed to go for the interview and subsequently did not even have the chance to get the job.

When I say, "Allow", I mean that I had the ability to go anywhere I wanted, whether Tiffany wanted it or not. The problem was, if I decided to do something she didn't like, she would go berserk, and then I had to live with the irrational anger and temper tantrums. Controllers use this behavior to get their way and keep things their way. I was not educated enough about the disorder to do things differently and not enable Tiffany.

Earlier in the year, just a few months before we found out we were having a baby, I started investigating the possibility of buying a franchised business. I was a good saver and had about twenty-five thousand dollars in my retirement account from the years of working two or three jobs all the time.

I sent a request for information to a fast food sandwich style restaurant and an income tax preparation company. I chose these two companies for two reasons. I had prior experience working in the food industry as well as the tax preparation business. Second reason was, they were two of the most economical businesses to get into.

Upon investigating further, I discovered that the startup costs were around seventy-five thousand at the time. Because I only had enough for the down payment, I hoped I'd be able to finance the rest. At that time, it was only a dream. I never realized it would actually happen. The dream was born a few years earlier when I began to think about it during the tax class I was taking at night. Little did I realize, I would someday open up six offices, in four different cities, with one of the largest tax preparation companies in America!

Several weeks passed, and while I never received a response to my inquiry from the restaurant franchise, I was contacted by the tax preparation franchise. They actually did a great job of contacting me and answering all of my concerns. They really made me feel comfortable with the idea of buying into their business. It was a huge decision for someone who was only twenty-four years old. I took a lot of time to think about it. I worried about the risks.

I knew if I tried and failed it would be devastating. How could I recover from such a failure? The fact that I was going to borrow a huge amount of money and possibly not be able to pay it back kept me up at night. Failure would mean I couldn't provide for my child and would not be able to give him all the wonderful things he deserved. Things like going to Disney World when he turned three or four, or being able to afford to build him a treehouse in the back yard. I wanted to give this little one the best of everything.

After learning that we were having a baby, I finally decided to risk it all. I sacrificed a guaranteed salary, a modest one, but guaranteed nonetheless, and risked losing what little money I had. It took ten years to earn and save that money. I was well aware that if I didn't do it, my son would not have much of a future.

A couple of months after deciding to purchase this franchise, Tiffany and I were on vacation in Illinois visiting my sister and her family. The tax preparation company sent the contract via Fed Ex to my sister's house, where we signed it. My hands were shaking as I wrote out the check. It was the biggest check I had ever signed. It was exciting, and scary, all at the same time. This was huge for someone who was only twenty-five years of age. Throughout the years since then, I have signed thousands of paychecks, and eventually signed checks in excess of one hundred thousand dollars, but that first time was the scariest.

My parents, Tiffany and I, drove up to Illinois together. While we were there, we had more tension and pressure erupt in our personal relationship. As we were driving, there were billboards up and down the highway advertising strip clubs and adult video stores. Each time we passed one of those signs, she would swear up and down that I was looking at the billboard with lewd imaginations. Because we had other people in the car, she tried to keep her rage to a low volume, and under control, so as not to alert anyone else of her irrational thoughts.

Just a few days later we went to the zoo. My sister wanted to take a picture of Tiffany and I together. For some crazy reason, Tiffany became angry, believing she was left out of the picture deliberately. Her wild thoughts led her to believe my sister had us sit down beside each other, just so she could snap a picture of only me. This episode led to a day of knock down, dragged out arguing, anger and misery. These quarrels kept everyone from having a joyous reunion.

Can you imagine living every moment of your day walking on eggshells? I never knew when the next episode of a volcanic eruption would take place. A co-worker that I ran into at the supermarket says, "Hi" and she flies off the handle. I compliment Tiffany on the new hair color she used, and she goes into a raging fit, asking me, "Oh, so you didn't like the color my hair was before this?". I say, "No honey, that's not what I said. I simply meant that I like the color that you dyed it right now."

There were times when we were watching a movie, and there would be a scene of a woman in a bra, or her underwear, and the accusations would start to fly. I only rented PG13 movies because of her jealousy and horrific allegations. What a sick, tortured way to live life! The saddest part of all was that the accusations were not true. The only one thinking those thoughts was Tiffany herself. All of this was a result of her Borderline Personality Disorder. It is a horrific mental illness that not only tortures the person that has it, but the people around them as well.

Chapter Six

Our New Life Together

We moved into the new house that we had built after returning home from our vacation. I had previously been living with my mom and dad. Tiffany was living with her sister, Julie, and Julie's husband, Kyle. Julie and Kyle were always quiet people. We never got in each other's way. We spent most of our time at their house while dating. It always reeked of marijuana. Kyle always smoked outside on the lanai. I was glad to get Tiffany out of that house. It wasn't good for her or our soon to be born baby to have her breathing in that second-hand smoke.

Our new home was small, about 1200 square feet, but it was brand new and beautiful. We chose a cranberry color scheme. The cabinets, paints and carpets all coordinated with our color scheme. Even the outside was painted a shade of cranberry that coordinated with what we decorated with on the inside. It was gorgeous, and it was ours.

What a special moment it is to move into your brand new first home. We went every other day to see how the building process was going. It was mesmerizing to see something go from a slab of concrete to an attractive, contemporary new home. Our neighbors across the street had taken pictures of our home throughout the process and gave them to us in a photo album as a welcome gift. It was so very nice of them.

What a great time we had shopping for furniture, silverware, curtains, dishes and all kinds of household items. If all of these things couldn't make Tiffany happy, then what could?

This house saw more than its fair share of grief and violence. During our short time we lived there, Tiffany would raise her fist to me, threatening to hit me. I am not saying this to put down my former partner but rather to expose how many men suffer violence and abuse behind closed doors.

If you are a man or woman living in such a relationship, there is hope. No one should have to live this way. You are certainly not alone. Silence about the abuse enables the enemy to continue.

Tiffany punched holes in the walls. She threw objects at me, making more holes, dents and scratches in the walls. Many times, when someone walks into a home and observes so many holes in the walls or doors, they assume the man is the violent one. Not always! One time, Tiffany, curled up her hand in a ball, threatening to punch me. I politely reminded her that while I would never attack anyone, that I would defend myself. I told her that if she hit me, I would hit back, and I reminded her that I could hit harder. That was the only thing that kept her from being physically abusive to me. My assurances that I would defend myself kept her in some kind of check. Tiffany would only hit and physically abuse people that wouldn't hit back, people that she could control through fear.

Usually, when someone is a bully, they remain that way or even get more spiteful, and confident, until another person stands up to them. If they remain silent about it, it will only increase the abuse.

Verbal abuse is another tactic abuser's use. Sometimes it is even worse because of the deep wounds it causes. It is a deliberate attack to methodically tear down its victim's self-esteem and confidence. In that way, verbal abuse causes the victim to have no self-esteem. That is why so many of the people living in such relationships stay so long or never leave. It has been pounded into them that they are worthless and deserve to be treated like a dog. Because of this cruel tactic, they have no strength to leave such an abusive, unhealthy relationship.

I do have to be honest and tell you, there were some great memories made in that house as well, it wasn't all bad. My son, Jonathan, was born while we lived there.

Jonathan was born several months after moving into our new home. He was born through a C-section on December second, two thousand and two. I was with Tiffany through the whole surgery. It was tough to watch them as they sliced open Tiffany's stomach. Then my jaw dropped as the doctor reached in and forcefully yanked my son out of his momma's belly. It appeared to me that the doctor was very barbaric and harsh with the way he handled my son. I didn't like it at all, but I also knew he did this all the time and he knew what he was doing. It was truly amazing. My son was a minute old and my protective, fatherly instinct were already operating at full force!

When I saw Jonathan for the first time, as the doctor was pulling him out, I saw that he had a full, thick head of beautiful, black hair. I yelled to Tiffany, "He's got hair, he's got hair, a full head of thick, black hair". I was beside myself, nervous, excited, happy, and frightened all at the same time. At that time, I never believed in the love at first sight thing. From the first moment I laid eyes on Jonathan, I loved him. I loved him more than I have ever loved anyone else on this earth.

He was my purpose in life, the reason I existed. I believe that God didn't create my son for me, but that God created me for my son. I know that God had chosen me specifically to be the father of this wonderful, little guy named Jonathan. What an honor it is, to be hand-picked by the Creator of the universe to be the dad of such an extraordinary child. The Lord has shared with me that Jonathan is destined to do great things in this world. I know God is shaping Jonathan into becoming a leader. One that will change the world.

This reminds me of a time just a couple of years after he was born, when Jonathan was three or four years old, we were sitting on the couch and I asked him what he wanted to do with his life when he was older. He told me, "Dad, I'm going to make a lot of money, and I'm going to use it to buy food for poor people, and buy them clothes, and I'm going to build houses for them". All of this came from the pure, generous heart of a three or four-year-old. I have never known any other child that had a plan to save the world at that age. I'm so proud of Jonathan and all that he is destined to become.

The nurses then brought Jonathan over to me on a little table. They handed me scissors to cut off the remaining umbilical cord. My little bundle of joy was crying so pitifully. The sound of his crying had a pattern to it. It would be one long cry, followed by three short cries. To this day I can still hear the sound of his cry and remember his voice just as it sounded on the first day. It was the greatest day of my life!

After I cut the umbilical cord, they took my son out of the operating room to wash him and dress him. The nurses had me follow them. I didn't want to leave Jonathan's side for a moment. While the nurse was bathing him, we chatted. She told me that typically you don't have to wash a baby's hair, because the vast majority of babies don't have any. Another medical person came in and had to prick Jonathan's heel for a blood sample. He let everyone know, he didn't like that. Finally, he was wrapped in a cloth, with a knitted hat on his head, and I sat there in a chair, holding him in my arms for the very first time. I memorized every little detail. He was nine pounds, seven point two ounces, and twenty-one and a half inches tall. His thick black hair framed his chubby angelic face, and his beautiful smiling blue eyes. It was the most exhilarating day of my life.

I do have a confession to make concerning this day. By this time in our relationship, I knew it wasn't going to last much longer. I knew it was not going to end well. Early in the morning, while I was waiting in the hallway for them to prep Tiffany for the C-section, I had prayed to God, asking Him to get me out of the situation I had gotten myself into. I prayed that He would let me leave the hospital with my son, and my son alone. I had actually prayed that Tiffany would not make it out alive. I had hoped that she would have some kind of medical complication and would not survive. I've heard of so many mothers dying during child birth due to some unexpected medical complications. In my heart, I had hoped that would happen to Tiffany.

After my son was born, they brought her into a recovery room for a few hours. I wasn't able to see her until they removed her from the recovery room and placed her into a regular hospital room. I watched the clock, and as every minute passed, I was hoping the doctor or nurse would come out to give me the news that something had gone wrong and she wasn't doing well. And as every minute passed, with no news of complications, I grew more anxious and disappointed.

In no way am I saying what I meditated on was correct. I am ashamed of entertaining those thoughts, but at the time I was in a really bad situation. I did not have hope for mine and Jonathan's lives and our future.

I didn't know what to do. Not having a relationship with God at the time, I did not have any moral compass as to what the right thing was to do. My shame and guilt kept me away from the One who loved and cared about me. That is not an excuse, it just shows how desperate someone can be when they have such an abusive person with wildly erratic mood swings in their life. I have nothing but regret for the horrible wishes I had at that time. I should have trusted God to deliver me from this awful dilemma. I have found that God's ways are always perfect. He makes a way where there is no way. Jesus referred to Himself as "The Way", and since I dedicated my life to the Lord, I have found this to be true. There is always a way when we invite the Lord into our lives.

Tiffany spent one or two nights in the hospital to recover from the surgery, and I slept on a couch in the hospital room with our son there as well. Changing his diaper for the very first time was scary. He was so tiny, and this little boy was so helpless. I fed him every hour and a half to two hours. The only way he could communicate was with a cry. He was depending on me to understand what he needed.

I remember bringing my little man home. Tiffany did not seem to have any maternal instincts, so I provided most of my son's care. I'd wake up several times each night to feed him and change his diaper, and then wake up to a twelve-hour work day. I didn't mind. I was working for a purpose. That little guy needed me to provide for him, and it was a joy to do so.

In addition to my son being born during our time there, I can also remember many other memories that I cherish while living at that house.

Each evening I'd lay down on the couch and read him children's Bible stories. I would fall asleep with him laying on my chest and he would fall asleep right there with me. It was a heavenly peace between the two of us that bonded us together forever.

Then there were some memories that make me laugh when I think of them. Like the time I had several computers on the living room floor, disassembled while I was repairing them. I was getting them ready for my first tax season with the franchise that I purchased. Jonathan had a wet diaper, so I laid him on the floor, took off his diaper, wiped and powdered him, and walked a few feet away to get a new diaper. A moment later, I turn around to see that he was peeing, and it was shooting straight up in the air, flying around in a circle and landing on one of my computers. It was a tender, funny moment a parent will hold dear to their heart forever.

Another time, I was changing his diaper, and I took off the poopy diaper, wiped him, and with my left hand I held onto his feet to hold his butt off of the floor. With my right hand, I reached for a diaper, and BOOM, in a split second he shot a blob of poop out of his butt. It went airborne, never hitting the ground, instead it flew and hit my right arm. It was hilarious, and I learned another lesson about parenting. The lesson is to always have the clean diaper and everything else you need close by and ready to go.

One other memorable moment we experienced at our new home was when my mom and sister came over with a few bags of groceries for us. At that time, our son had just been born and Tiffany wasn't working because she just had a C-section. Neither of us were making any money. I had just opened my first tax preparation office and was years away from turning a profit.

We were buying food and putting gas in our cars with my credit cards. I would use the convenience checks that the banks would send out in your monthly statements in order to borrow money from my credit cards to pay our mortgage and utility bills. I had just used half of the twenty-five thousand I had saved to buy a new car because my old one had broken down.

The other half was used as the down payment for the initial franchise fee for the business. I also had to borrow tens of thousands of dollars on my cards to get my office up and running. I'd use cards that offered the low introductory rate, and when that rate expired, I would transfer the balance to another card offering a zero or low percentage rate. I would continue to juggle the debt, moving from one card to another to try to minimize the growth of the debt.

We had no actual cash and were very deep in debt. We would cook fifty cent boxes of spaghetti for dinner one night of the week and alternate with Kraft macaroni and cheese the next night. Once a week we treated ourselves to a couple of hot dogs chopped up and added to the mac and cheese. On spaghetti night we used butter on the pasta because we just didn't have the money to buy spaghetti sauce. It was the only time in my life that I was poor, really poor. Despite the tough times, God still provided us with a roof over our heads, and food on the table.

I will never forget the act of kindness and generosity from my mother and sister. It may only have been fifty- or sixty-dollars' worth of food, but it came when we had absolutely nothing! It has been many years since, and I have never again experienced lack, nor has anyone in my family. God always provided, no matter what the situation looked like in the natural realm.

Chapter Seven
Sleeping with The Enemy

We celebrated Jonathan's first Christmas at our new home, with all of Tiffany's family coming over in the morning for a great meal and presents. My family came over in the evening. After we ate, we sat down and opened presents. Tiffany was still a little sluggish from the surgery two weeks before. I was also sleep deprived and in a constant battle of indecision and fear, so much so that I don't even remember what any of the presents were.

Two weeks after Christmas, I opened my first income tax preparation office at the mall. I had rented a space right across from the food court, and right next to a popular restaurant. I was lucky to have my father renovating the space with me and converting it to an office. My talents and skills were limited to management and finances. I was not a handyman at all. Fortunately for me though, my dad was very handy. I will never forget the hard work he did to help me start the business. I could never have done it on my own. My dad knew I didn't have the money to hire contractors and laborers.

He worked a three to eleven p.m. shift at the hospital as a cook. From 9:00 AM until 2:00 PM, he installed paneling, laid down carpet, installed light fixtures, and basically helped me build my dream.

As the relationship with Tiffany continued to deteriorate, I realized that I needed to do something. It was now January 2003, and I was determined to protect my little boy, so I started going through the phone book to find an attorney. Over the course of a few days, I had spoken to three attorneys on the phone. Two were female and one was male. The one thing they all had in common was that they all gave me the same advice. If I ever wanted to see my son again, I should stay with her, give her what she wants, and keep her happy. They did not even try to take my money. They were actually "honest" attorneys! They told me how courts always give the children to their mothers, and how few legal rights dads have concerning their children. It did not seem fair. It seemed like discrimination, but that's the way it was.

It was in late January that I went to see Attorney Michael Anderson. I don't remember the conversation at all, but I did not hire him then because I was afraid of what would happen if I did so. Michael was a great attorney, honest and fair. I would end up using him several times over the course of almost fourteen years.

In addition to all the issues she had, Tiffany also had a fear of being alone. While I was working, she would take our son to her mom's house, and come home later when I came home from work. I didn't want that! Her mom and stepdad smoked, and my son would have to breathe in the second-hand smoke all day. In fact, when she brought Jonathan home, he stank of cigarette smoke. I suspected that her parents were drug addicts. Later on, my suspicions were confirmed. I hated that my son was exposed continually to the smoke, drugs and instability, but as I would soon find out, there was nothing I could do to keep Jonathan from it.

The insanity was increasing by the day. At this time, I actually began to fear for my life. I never felt she would harm our son, but I was very worried about Tiffany hurting me or herself. I couldn't stand to be around her, so I started sleeping in a spare bedroom. One particular night stands out in my memory. I woke up and was half asleep, I barely opened my eyes when I saw Tiffany standing over me just staring, not saying a word. I was so exhausted with all of my work and a brand-new baby, that I just fell back asleep. When I woke up in the morning, I remembered what had happened, and it scared me! It seemed like something you see in a movie when a crazy killer strikes their victim in their sleep. After that night, I started to take all the knives and sharp objects in the house and lock them up in the spare bedroom with me while I slept.

The fears that I started having for my safety were not unmerited. Tiffany had a scar on her left wrist, and she was right handed, so I presumed it was from a past suicide attempt. Also, I had seen Tiffany take things like forks and butter knives to try to cut herself when she was in a rage. I knew she had the potential to be dangerous to herself, or me.

Tiffany continued to act in a menacing fashion throughout all of tax season, especially when a young woman came in looking for a job. I hired her. I had no choice, I needed employees to run the office, and she had experience. Quite honestly, it didn't matter. If I hired a man, she would accuse me of being gay, and sleeping with him. The same thing happened with women. I think that if I had bought a puppy, she probably would have had some awful things to say about my relationship with the puppy.

She didn't live in the reality that you and I live in. Her mind would create an alternative reality, and that reality was always the truth in her mind. She was a pathological liar. The vast majority of things that came out of her mouth were fantasy. I would catch her lying all the time. When she would make up a lie, awhile later we would be talking about the same topic, and she would give a totally different story. Every time she told a story it was different. She would forget what lie she told me before and make up a new one when discussing the same topic.

I can't help but to think that the story of my relationship with her would make one heck of a movie. It would certainly be a thriller with all its twists and turns. Living it was hell on earth. Tiffany reminds me of the crazy girlfriends in movies like, Swim Fan, My Crazy Super Ex-Girlfriend or like the woman in Fatal Attraction. All these movies are based upon characters with Borderline Personality Disorder. This mental illness is much less known than things like bi-polar, and schizophrenia. By no means am I criticizing anyone with mental illness. I am simply describing what I dealt with. The real-life characteristics and actual events are something I and my son actually lived through. I would encourage anyone living this way to seek help for themselves or the loved one that needs help.

I actually talked to Tiffany's sisters in February 2003 about it. They all agreed that she needed psychological treatment because of the pain and suffering she and her siblings endured at the hands of their biological father, as he molested, raped, and brutalized them all when they were young children.

Her biological father had a criminal record a mile long. I would have to add several chapters to this book just to list the crimes he had committed. Things like burglary, arson, drugs, etc.

There were other crimes he committed that he was never convicted of such as, child abuse, rape and according to Tiffany, murder. He passed away in the late nineties. Tiffany described his death as a murder that was made to look like suicide. As a drug dealer, you either end up in prison or dead.

They also made me aware that Tiffany and her step dad also had some violent arguments that included, hurling things at him, punching him, and actually throwing a chair at him. The chair hit him on the head, and he had the scars to prove it!

Tiffany's sisters agreed to meet with her to try to talk her into getting some help. After meeting with her sisters, she agreed to begin treatment with a mental health care professional. As the weeks went by, I'd ask her over and over again if she had made an appointment with a mental health care professional, but she would simply give me one excuse after another, about why she hadn't done it yet.

Tiffany would say things like, "I can't find anyone who takes my health insurance. I would then hand her my credit card and say, "Here, I'll pay for it". The excuses continued as her sisters and I pleaded with her to get help. After weeks of refusing to go, I tried to persuade her sisters to Baker Act Tiffany. The Baker Act is a Florida law that relatives, spouses and friends can use to have their loved ones committed to a psychiatric facility for help if they deem their loved one is a threat to themselves or others. Her sister Rebecca was not comfortable with doing that and would not agree. So, there was nothing more that could be done. Something as simple as forcing her to get a psychological evaluation would have been monumental in terms of protecting myself and my son. At this point, I had no choice but to finally give her an ultimatum, to either begin treatment, or our relationship would end.

As the weeks continued to pass, I wanted out, but I could not leave because of my son. One night at work, I ended up talking to the young woman that worked for me, and she invited me to come and spend the night at her place. I told her I couldn't, and I had to go home to my son. I was still in a relationship with Tiffany, and had never been unfaithful before, and I wasn't about to start now. I was once told that my loyalty and faithfulness were my strengths, but they were also my greatest weaknesses, because those traits kept me in a relationship that was unhealthy for me and my son.

It wasn't easy having a female working at the office for me. I remember one time having this young woman call me to ask a question about how to do something at the office. Operating as many as six offices throughout the southwest region of Florida, I can tell you that it isn't uncommon for me to receive fifty to one hundred calls a day from my employees, asking me how to do this or that. Tiffany and I were at home when I answered the phone and oh boy, was she mad! She sat there listening to every word spoken. When I finally hung up the phone, World War Three broke out! Actually, at this point in time, I think we could've called it World War nine hundred and seventy-two. The battles would rage on for years and years, even after our relationship ended.

I remember this employee, Jessica, telling me that she had seen a woman walking back and forth through the mall, passing by the office many times, staring into the office with a furious look on her face. Jessica told me this happened on several occasions. One day Tiffany actually came into the office and asked her where I was. She told Tiffany that I went to the bank to make a deposit, which is where I really was.

When I went home, it was hell again. The questions flew at a machine gun pace. "Where were you? You told me you were working. When I went to the office you weren't there. That whore told me you were at the bank. I want the truth. Where were you? Don't tell me anymore lies! I want the truth." Tiffany's face was purple with rage as she continued screaming and violently throwing things.

Almost every day the same scenario took place. First, the verbal rampage, then came the physical. There was hysteria, screaming, and throwing things. This was pretty much what went on every day. This reminds me of a movie called Groundhog Day, starring Bill Murray. In the movie, Bill Murray keeps reliving a horrible day, over and over and over. With the movie, it got more and more hilarious each day. Unfortunately, I relived the same day over and over, but nothing about what I was living was funny.

Chapter Eight
Abduction

It was March 11, 2003. I was at work when Tiffany walked into the mall. It wasn't busy. Tax season usually slows down by the end of February. Most people had already rushed in to get their refunds. I was sitting at the desk in front of the computer when Tiffany came in with Jonathan in his stroller.

I don't remember everything we talked about, but it was a very tense atmosphere. All I remember is that we were talking about the bills. I reminded her that her car payment was due in a few days and to remember to pay it. She blew up at me and started screaming. Thankfully, there was no one else in the office. It would have been both humiliating and bad for business if a customer saw the whole sick scene.

I have never acted anything but professionally in all my work places. I was horrified that she would carry on like this when she knew it was our family's livelihood. By this time, I was so tired of the insanity, I was completely worn out. I was sitting down, and I slammed my hand down hard on my desk, and with a very strong commanding voice, told her to leave the office. Tiffany took Jonathan and left. It was as they say, the last straw that broke the camel's back. I had not had a full night's sleep for months, and when I left work, I faced piles of laundry, grocery shopping and full-time care of an infant. I had no idea that my life was about to change forever. I didn't know this would be the last time I would see my son for sixty-six long days and nights. I didn't have an inkling of what agony and suffering me, and Jonathan would go through.

After the argument in the office, Tiffany took our son to her mom's house for several days. I had talked to her on the phone, cautiously trying to persuade her to come back to our house. I reminded Tiffany that she and her sisters agreed that she would seek counseling, and that I would be with her every step of the way. The only thing she would agree to, was to have me go to her mom's house to see our son. I feared for my life, so I would not go alone. I told her I would bring my dad with me, but she refused.

I was told to come alone or not at all. It was obvious what she was trying to do. I knew if I agreed I probably wouldn't be alive to tell this story. My counter offer was to meet with her in a public place. Once again Tiffany refused and demanded I go to her mom's house by myself.

I know you must be wondering, what about Child Protective Services? What about the police? Tiffany married a police officer after our split. When you have a cop married to your ex, it is easy for them to cover up things and to get special favors from other corrupt cops.

Unfortunately, I was not aware how much dishonesty and bribery there is in local police departments, child protective services and other government agencies. In the meantime, precious time with my son kept being denied.

In the state of Florida, the state constitution guarantees every citizen should be treated the same, regardless of age, religion, and gender. I was not treated that way. I signed the birth certificate, legally establishing that I was the father, but I still had no rights to visitation with my son without a court order. I still had the financial responsibility but no visitation with Jonathan. No, I am not a lawyer, but common sense would indicate these laws are indeed discriminatory against one specific gender, which in fact, violates the state constitution itself. I spent years challenging these laws, but ultimately to no avail.

Days turned into weeks, and weeks turned into months since I had seen my son. My mom and sister came into the office one day. We were discussing my legal battles. My mother had experienced this before with my brother. He was in a relationship with a teenage mom very similar to Tiffany. My mom saw the handwriting on the wall. She knew that Tiffany would try to destroy me, so her advice was to leave the state of Florida in order to save my own life. My mom felt I would not be safe remaining in Florida. She pleaded with me to run. My mother was aware of the fights, and of Tiffany's violent behavior.

I responded to her with one statement, and one statement only. "There is no man, woman, child or beast on the face of God's green earth, that will ever tear down this house." I said this without thought, without the tiniest bit of fear in my body or soul. My mother did not understand, and so my sister explained to her what I meant by "This house". "This house" that I described was my life, my business, my family and most importantly, my son.

The one thing I had never told my mom and sister, when I told them that "There is no man, women, child or beast on the face of God's green earth, that will ever tear down this house", is why "This house" could never be torn down. And that is simply because "This house", is the house that God built. My staying and my surviving have led to the fulfillment of God's plan for my life.

It was at that moment that I declared the will of God over my life. It was His will that I fight the good fight of faith. What was at stake was the life of my son, an innocent victim. None of this was his fault. It was mine.

In hindsight I wonder, "What if" I could go back in time? Knowing what I know now, would I go back and stay with her in order to protect my son from years of physical and emotional abuse? Would it have made it easier for her to kill me, leaving my son with no one to protect him? I'll never know what would have happened if I stayed with Tiffany. What I do know is that it would begin more than a decade of lies, false accusations, stalking, harassment and even an attempt to take my life. My family always had to sleep with one eye open, and Jonathan had to live his life in fear.

A characteristic of Borderline Personality Disorder is fear of abandonment and rejection. The person with BPD will come after you if they feel as though you abandoned or rejected them. The BPD person will be relentless. They will spend the rest of their lives on this earth, chasing down the person whom they claim to love. Then, they will try to destroy the person.

It's kind of like hunting. I've never been hunting, but from what I have been told, it is just a game for fun, for ones' own amusement. The animals never did anything to you, but they just happen to be there, and you happen to want to kill them. That is just the way it works. An individual who "abandons" or "rejects" the person with BPD, often becomes the focus of their obsession.

When this happens, they obsess over their "game" constantly. They become angry that they cannot have the person they were in relationship with. They cannot have their victim, so no one else should have them either. It is quite common for them to start a smear campaign against their prey.

Tiffany did this immediately after the break-up. I worked at another income tax preparation company two years earlier and had just purchased my tax preparation franchise. Signing a non-compete agreement is standard practice in this industry. The non-compete agreement I had with my former employer had a few more months in it before it expired. The agreement legally restricts a former employee from taking customer lists. It also bans an employee from directly contacting the customers they had at their former place of business.

The non-compete agreement does not restrict you from opening an office, and/or advertising to the public to acquire new clients. A past employee is not allowed to steal the customer sales list from the earlier employer. The first thing Tiffany and her mom did, was to contact my past employer and tell them I was trying to steal away their clients. The office manager called me to let me know. It was mortifying, debasing and totally untrue. This was Tiffany's first attempt to destroy my business, but it certainly would not be the last...

When Tiffany saw her plan didn't work, she sent her step dad to vandalize our kiosk inside Walmart. I got a phone call one morning during tax season from one of my employees telling me the work kiosk was damaged and torn apart. I drove down to see what happened. Sure enough, our computers, printers, and furniture were all knocked around, some of it totally destroyed. I knew immediately who did it. So, I went to talk to several Walmart associates, and found the security cameras did not cover the area where our kiosk was located.

I had shown a picture of her step dad to several employees that worked the night before, and many of them identified him as someone they saw by the kiosk. He went to the customer service asking questions like, "When does the tax service open?" or "Why isn't anyone working here now?" Because the security cameras didn't record it, there was nothing I could do.

There were many more things like this that would happen throughout the years. One of the more memorable attacks against my business was when she sent an acquaintance of hers to get a job with my company, with the purpose of damaging it. One of my employees told me that a gentleman I hired, Bob Adams, was being incredibly rude and disrespectful to clients, telling them to leave the office, and that he could not assist them.

At first, I didn't accept it because he appeared to be intelligent and an all-around nice guy. One day I was sitting down chatting with him, making small talk. I asked him how his wife was doing, what type of work did she do, etc... Bob slipped up and wound up telling me that his wife worked at the same company Tiffany was working at. I remained calm and acted unmoved by this revelation. We continued our conversation, and when he left, I changed the lock to the office door, disabled his access to the company's computer database, and then fired him!

Perhaps you are thinking, who in the world would be crazy enough to send a "spy" to their ex-boyfriend's business to try to destroy it? Then the next question would be, who in the world is crazy enough to actually be the "spy" that agrees to do it?

Let's look at this a little closer. Let's say you are the older gentleman, whose wife works in an office with your former partner, and your wife comes home and tells you that her co-worker is looking to find someone to get a job with her ex, so she can find a way to ruin his business. Your wife tries to talk you into it, and you agree! It's called crazy on steroids. I'm sitting here, still trying to figure out which one is crazier, the old man for doing it, his wife who asked him to do this, or the woman who asked her co-worker to participate in her evil plot to annihilate my tax preparation franchise? It's a tossup. Any one of them could win this one!

At any rate, I can see the hand of God protecting mine and Jonathan's future. What are the odds that workers would come and tell their boss someone is trying to demolish their boss' business? Furthermore, that the man trying to betray him, would let it slip that his wife and my ex were working together? In addition to that, God gave me the wisdom to actually know what to do, and the problem-solving skills to know by what means to do it. How I thank God for His protection and wisdom! Even when I wasn't praying or following God, He was guiding me.

Chapter Nine

But God?

Many times, people don't realize why God tells us to do certain things, but then tells us not to do other things. It's not that He wishes to control us. He created us with a free will, to make our own decisions. However, He knows where our bad choices will lead us. That is the reason He tries to guide us down the path of righteousness, making godly decisions based on His word. It's not so we won't have any fun in this life, but so that we won't have to suffer the consequences of our sins. Sometimes, like in my case, not only did I suffer the results of my sins, but an innocent child, my son, also had to suffer because of my sinful choices. This is something I will have to live with the rest of my life. I am aware that I deserve to burn in the flames of hell for all eternity. But thanks to what Jesus did on the cross two thousand years ago, my sin has already been paid for. Even though I committed the sin, Jesus paid the penalty. By the grace of God, I am forgiven and treated as though I have never sinned. While my son and I carry the scars, we can be certain that we have new life through a relationship with God's son, Jesus.

I can look back on my life now and see how starting this business was a part of God's plan for my life. During the eighteen months after signing the contract and starting the business, my debt had accumulated into the six-figure range. This debt included the initial start-up costs for the business, everyday living expenses, and so much more. I felt like I was drowning. There was no way I could get out of the financial hole I was in.

I was considering either the sale of the business, or bankruptcy. I thought these were my only options, the only way to climb out from underneath the back-breaking financial load I was carrying. I felt like I was facing my own financial Armageddon.

I found a buyer for my business in the summer of 2004. However, it was in December 2004, that I received a letter from the buyer, stating that he had changed his mind and decided not to move forward with the purchase. He said he felt as though it wasn't a good time for him to expand his business at the time. After reading it, I was heart-broken. I was looking forward to being able to get out of debt. Looking back, I can easily see how it was the hand of God that stopped me from making one of the biggest mistakes of my life.

From 2003 until 2005, I didn't earn a single penny in profits from all of my labor, and all of my sacrifices. After all of these years of hard work and dedication, in 2006, God's blessings began to pour into my life. I earned $150,000 that year. God knew what He was doing. He had everything under control. His timing was perfect. It was later in 2006 that my dad had fallen ill, and became disabled, and wasn't able to work anymore. My dad's need came as no surprise to God. His plan to provide was in place long before my dad's disability ever happened. It was by God's grace, that I was able to begin taking care of my disabled parents when I was twenty-nine years old.

Just a few years later, by the time I was in my early thirties, I paid off my house. Before the age of forty I wrote out a hefty check to buy an RV and travel the country. How amazing God is!

If we trust God and allow Him to be in control, what blessings will come! He will cause you to make wise choices and bring you to places you would never have gone on your own. I am so thankful to God for the many miracles He has given me.

If I had chosen to push away God's guidance, you would not be reading about God's promises fulfilled. I lived all these years with hope, hope that made no sense. This hope defied reality. It also caused me to develop my faith, when in the natural I should have given up. I could have buried my problems in a bottle of alcohol or chosen to drug my way through the pain, but by the grace of God, I didn't.

I prayed and asked God for forgiveness and He gave it to me. I shudder to think what might have happened if I had been proud and refused God's guidance. I have a great life now. It didn't change instantly, but it did change. The Word says, all His paths are paths of peace. That means that as you seek God and ask Him to guide you, even if there is hell breaking loose all around you, you can still have peace in the midst of it, and eventually you will be living the life you desired. He grants His loved ones their heart's desire when they stay firmly planted in His kingdom.

Chapter Ten

The Cross

Years ago, my brother had a baby girl named Monica with his sixteen-year-old girlfriend. Shortly after the birth of their child, they ended their relationship. My niece, Monica, would spend the weekends with my brother and the rest of our family. My mom and I would go to pick Monica up on Fridays while my brother working.

When the little girl would come to us, she would have filth caked on her skin and hair. In spite of the way she was treated she had such a sweet personality, and she especially loved to be cuddled and happily played peek-a-boo with anyone willing to do so. I adored my little niece.

When she would visit with us the first thing my mom would do was to give her a bath. While giving her a bath one Friday afternoon after picking her up, my mom saw cigarette burns all over her body. Mom took her to the pediatrician, who confirmed that they appeared to be cigarette burns. The doctor contacted Child protective services and had her admitted to the hospital for evaluation. The investigators came in, did their investigation and in the end, the child went home with her mother. It seems to me that the mothers always get the children, no matter how bad a parent they are.

After that incident my brother and our family moved to Illinois, where my brother would never see her again. Shortly after moving, I remember as a twelve-year-old boy, hearing the voice of God in my little soul, promising me that someday I would go back and find her. It wasn't until several years later, as an eighteen-year-old, I remembered the promise, and I began to search for her on my own.

When I did this, I felt compelled to buy her a 14K gold cross and necklace. When I purchased it, I had my niece's name engraved down the middle, and her date of birth on the left-hand side. The day she was born was up to that point the greatest day of my life. I left the right side of the cross blank to someday put the day she would come back into our lives.

My intention was to eventually give it to her as a gift. It was meant to be a tangible reminder of the promise God made me when I was twelve-years old. It would be a symbol of hope, believing God would bring her back. Many years later that promise was fulfilled.

In March 2003, after Tiffany had taken my son, I once again heard God's s voice in my soul, as He made me the promise that He would someday bring my baby home. So again, I bought a cross, had Jonathan's name engraved on it. The greatest day of my life, the date of his birth, was engraved on the left side of the cross. I left the right side of the cross blank to record the second most wonderful day of my life, which would be the day when Jonathan would finally come home to stay.

I often wonder why it took so long. For what purpose could God have for leaving my son to be scared and abused? How could it serve any meaningful purpose? To this day, I'm not sure. If God had brought Jonathan home sooner, there would not have been all the pain and suffering. There would have been a better chance of healing. I don't know why. This side of heaven there are many questions left unanswered. I have learned to trust Him, and honestly, I could never have gone through this without His presence and assurance in my life. It declares in the Bible, Numbers 23:19, "God is not a man that He should lie, neither the son of man that He would change His mind. Has He said, and will He not do it? Has He promised, and will He not fulfill?"

This is one of my favorite scriptures because it describes the true character of God, and it also is what gave me strength to endure throughout the years. It taught me what a promise is. It taught me that a promise is just like God Himself. It is forever.

Chapter Eleven
Legally Blind

After weeks of not seeing my son, I started to interview one attorney after another. I found one that wasn't like most of the others. His name was Todd Peterson. Mr. Peterson was very optimistic, unlike all the other attorneys I met. He was a glass half full kind of person. It was that optimistic and confident nature that led me to hire him. Most of the other attorneys didn't offer me any hope. They all told me that because of my gender, and considering the discrimination in the courts against fathers, that I would probably see my son twice a week for two hours each "visit".

That was simply unacceptable to me. Fathers were reduced to being nothing more than their children's visitors. We were used by the courts for money and treated like nothing more than paychecks. Each district of the court even went so far as to put into writing the "Parenting Guidelines" that dictated that non-custodial parents, fathers, were allowed to see their children on Tuesdays and Thursdays from 4-6pm, and every other Friday at 6:00 p.m. to Sunday morning at 11am. The court system wasn't even embarrassed or ashamed of the blatant discrimination.

Right before I met Todd Peterson, I had gone to an agency called Florida Rural Legal Association, funded by Florida taxpayers to provide free legal assistance to those that couldn't afford it. When I walked into their office in early April 2003, I had no money, and I wasn't earning anything at my tax business. They told me they had too many cases, they couldn't help me, and that they would put my name on a waiting list. A week later, I received a letter from them telling me that they took my name off of the list because the opposing party, my son's mother, had gone in and obtained free legal assistance from their office. They refused to help me, but a week later, they offered her a free attorney. Does that make any sense?

Mr. Peterson began instructing me on how to prepare for the case. He asked whether I had a crib, stroller, car seat, and all the other baby accessories that you would need. I told him I had already purchased all those things, but that his mother had taken them all. So, he told me to go ahead and buy it all again and to take pictures to give to him, so he could show the judge that I was prepared to care for my son.

After the petition for custody was served, his mother had twenty days to respond, and she did so through the attorney that the Florida Rural Legal Association had given her for free. I didn't have a clue what was going on. I received bill after bill from the attorney's office and wrote out checks borrowed from my credit cards. Each month I grew deeper and deeper into debt. I never even stopped to count all the money I was spending. It ended up at more than $25,000. I remember being so scared that I would call him to ask him about every little detail and to tell him every little thing, not realizing that I was being charged for every single phone call at quarter hour increments at $210 an hour. Ouch! That hurt.

After not seeing my son for sixty-six days and nights, the attorneys agreed to allow for "visitation" on Tuesdays and Thursdays from 4-6pm. I will never forget the first time we picked him up. It was at a fast-food restaurant. We met Tiffany's mom and stepdad inside. Her stepdad, George, was high as a kite. George's eyes were bloodshot, and his speech was slurred, and his gait was tilted and clumsy, all while he was holding my baby!

My mom and dad had gone with me to pick him up. After picking Jonathan up we went back to my parent's home, where my siblings and their spouses were anxiously awaiting my sons' arrival. It had been more than two-and-a-half months since they last saw Jonathan.

The first thing I did was to look for the red birthmark I knew he had on the back of his neck, just under his hair at the very bottom.   I hadn't seen him in such a long time, and he had changed so much, that I had to see and make sure it was him. He had the chubbiest cheeks you have ever seen, and the most beautiful blue eyes. His hair was dark black, and curly.

Jonathan had some bald spots on the back of his head, which I think was from being left to lay in the crib by himself for too long each day. I remember his diaper was soaked. He had a bad rash from sitting in the wet diaper too long. We all spent some time with him, and eventually, my sister gathered everyone together to leave, so I could spend some time alone with him.

Now the "visitation" lasted one week before Tiffany refused to allow me to see my son again. So, my attorney had to schedule an emergency hearing in front of Judge Peter Jones. I met with my attorney, and we walked in to the courtroom.   Tiffany's attorney at the time was Mr. Smith. The court session began, and my attorney, Mr. Peterson, introduced me to the court, and explained what was happening, and why we were there. He told the judge that Tiffany had denied me contact with our son for two-and-a-half months, and that he was requesting that the court would order "visitation", to prevent her from continuing to deny me contact.

At this point, after listening to Mr. Peterson describe how she maliciously interfered with my "visitation" rights, I was in tears. I missed my baby so much, and I was afraid that I wouldn't be able to be in his life. Her attorney responded by stating that Mr. Peterson's allegations weren't true, and that his client had never denied me contact with our son. Mr. Peterson and I had all the evidence to prove it, letters that I sent her via certified mail requesting to see my son, and even letter's that Mr. Peterson had sent to her via certified mail, and her attorney denied everything.

The judge was able to see right through the lies and in a swift and commanding voice he said, "Tiffany, the father has rights too." Then he continued to say, "You know he can't be denied overnight visitation, so I'd suggest Mr. Smith and Mr. Peterson work something out. I'll leave you alone to talk for a couple of minutes."

At this time, the judge walked out of the courtroom, and Mr. Smith and Mr. Peterson started talking about a proposed temporary visitation schedule. I was feeling pretty good at this moment, after the judge scolded her for her behavior. But then, the courts bailiff stepped out of the judge's chambers and whispered to the attorneys, Mr. Peterson later told me that the bailiff told them that the judge wanted to remind them to adhere to the courts "Parenting Guidelines", which is the courts "written rules" on family law that states that a father can only see his children twice a week for a couple of hours, and then every other Friday through Sunday morning. So, the attorneys ended up agreeing to visitation time on Tuesdays and Thursdays from 2 to 6 p.m. and every other Saturday from 1p.m. till Sunday at 11 am.

I finally had a small sense of relief, now that we had something in writing from the court guaranteeing me some time with my son. And to think, it only cost me $25,000 in legal fees to see my son!

Now I know why so many fathers end up leaving their children behind and becoming "deadbeats" as the system so likes to call them. It's simply because when you start out with no rights, because of the gender that God made you, and if you don't have $25,000 laying around under the mattress or buried in the backyard, you will never see your children again. It's that simple. Case closed.

She's a woman and you're a man, you lose. Period. It's hopeless. No one cares about what is in the best interest of the child. I'm not saying this is how it is in every state and I'm not saying that this is how it is today. I'm simply telling you how it was in 2003, in the state of Florida.

I even worked as a volunteer of the court as a Guardian Ad Litem for about a year. As a Guardian Ad Litem, you visit children that are in foster care, that have been taken from their families due to alleged abuse and neglect. The court sometimes orders Guardian Ad Litems for custody cases, like the one I was going through, in order to have the Guardian ad Litem act as a third party, neutral representative of the child. The Guardian Ad Litem is intended to act as the voice of the children.

Working on the inside gave me a bird's-eye view of the corruption. I won't comment further on the things I saw, but I couldn't continue being around this kind of lunacy. No matter what I did as a volunteer, the children would always be the ones that suffered, and I couldn't continue watching it. I quit after about a year.

What's unfortunate is that the entire system is defective. All the way from the broken laws to the court system that further aids and abets in the cruel business of separating children from their fathers. The only things that matter to anyone is the power and the money. The money that is funneled through the system, to the lawyers, whose children we put through private school, and through college. The judges sitting on the bench making six-figure salaries. The politicians work tirelessly, not to do what's in your best interest, but to do what's in their best interest. Their sole desire is to preserve their own power, no matter what the price. Because the majority of voters in America are women, the legislators would never do anything to upset them, especially pass a bill that would guarantee both parents equal rights.

Equal rights should mean equal parenting time. That would mean less money being transferred from one parent to another in what is typically referenced to as child support. I'm not against the thirty-four billion dollar a year business of child support at all. I recognize the need for BOTH parents to contribute to the lives of their children, in ALL ways, not just the ways that the court wishes to designate. In other words, it simply isn't right for one gender to always get custody and the other gender always gets "visitation".

It also isn't right that one parent provides for most of the child's financial needs alone, without a significant contribution from the child's other parent. Basically, the courts like to select one parent to be the primary care giver, and the other parent to be the primary financial provider. This simply isn't right. The courts like to impose their old fashioned, out of date, gender stereotypes onto families here in America, with a one size fit's all mentality. There are never two cases that are alike. In some cases, the mom is the better care giver, and in others, it's the dad. In some cases, the dad is more capable of providing financially for their children, and in other cases, it's the mother.

How is it the court's place to say that all women should be at home, bare foot and pregnant, cooking and cleaning and serving the needs of the family from home? Today, the reality is that women can choose to be a stay at home mom or have a career. There are women who choose to be pilots, politicians, lawyers, doctors and anything else they wish to be. How is it the court's place to determine that all men are incapable of caring for their children? How is it that the courts can determine that all men belong outside of the home, working, and doing nothing more than being a paycheck to their families?

This is how the courts operated fifteen plus years ago. It's the 21st century for goodness sake, and the courts are living with an early 20th century mentality. It hurts the children, by taking their fathers out of their lives and it hurts the dads that end up losing everything, including their kids, their money, and their parenthood. Instead, parents should be allowed to co-parent their children, with equal access to their kids, and equal responsibility.

Please understand that I realize that everyone's circumstances are different and that the situation I described above is what I experienced. In other cases, the variables and outcome could be different. All in all, all I'm advocating for is gender equality in our family courts.

Week after week passed after the emergency court hearing, and every time I went to pick up and drop off my son, I would bring a family member to ensure my safety. Every single time we met to exchange our son, there would always be chaos. I would remain silent, and mind my business, however, she wasn't capable of doing the same. Tiffany would always start yelling, screaming, throwing things, threatening us each time we met to exchange our son. She did all of this in front of our son.

She would usually bring her mom or step dad with her. After several weeks of being harassed, threatened, and assaulted, I decided to bring a video camera with the hope that she would start behaving. She saw the camera and knew the exchange of our son was being recorded. Yet Tiffany continued to harass us, threaten us, and throw things at us. I thought having it on video would in some way allow me the opportunity to seek legal protection from her. I got a lot of interesting stuff on camera, including her mom throwing things at us and her sister hitting the camera out of my hand. Usually, I would just leave the camera on the roof of the car, except one time I held it in my hand when her sister assaulted me.

Chapter Twelve
Bogus Restraining Order

It didn't take long for Tiffany and her mom to come up with a plan to do something dirty and untrue. In the Florida statutes, at the time this had happened, there was language that stated that if one of the parents had ever been arrested for domestic violence that they would be prohibited from having custody. After realizing this, she decided to try to set me up for a bogus restraining order.

In August 2003, I was at the mall having lunch when I received a call from her. She told me that our son was sick with a 104-degree fever and had diarrhea and was vomiting. She told me she wanted to let me know she was taking him to the hospital. I immediately called my parents so they could go with me. About thirty minutes later I arrived at the hospital with my mom and dad. Tiffany was already there in the waiting room with her mom. She had checked him in and we sat there and waited. After waiting about a half hour, the doctors finally took our son to a room.

The hospital did blood work, took his temperature, and monitored him for about two hours. Surprisingly, the doctor notated on the medical report that our son didn't have a fever when he first came in, nor did he have a fever at any other time during the two hours that they monitored him. According to the doctor, as noted on the medical report, our son didn't vomit, nor did he have diarrhea at all while at the hospital under observation. The blood work came back fine, and he was in perfect health.

The nurse had taken Tiffany and her mom back to see him and my parents and I were going to go see him when they were finished. Being in the same room with her was not wise because of her erratic behavior. So, my parents and I were sitting in the waiting room, and after about 15 minutes had passed, Tiffany didn't come out, so we went to the nurses' station to inquire about the status of my son. The nurse told me they had just left a few minutes ago, exiting out of the back door.

Tiffany left with our son never telling me. The hospital visit was simply staged for some other purpose. Our son was never sick. At the time, of course, I didn't know I was being set up for something. It wasn't until the next day that I found out what was going on. I was driving in my car the next evening, when my brother-in-law called me, and told me that the police were looking for me. I asked him what for and he said they needed to serve me with a restraining order.

I called the sheriff's office to inquire about it. They looked up my name on the computer and found that a restraining order had been filed against me earlier that morning. The sheriff's office advised me to head home and they would meet me there to deliver the documents to me. I came home and met with the sheriff's officer. He served me with the documents and explained to me what I could expect next. He informed me that the court will set a date for a hearing in front of a judge within fifteen days and until then I wouldn't be allowed to be within one hundred yards of Tiffany.

That meant that I couldn't participate with the exchange to see my son for the next fifteen days, and my parents would have to do so. The next morning, I contacted my attorney and made an appointment to meet with him. He advised me that when we meet in the courtroom to have the hearing on the restraining order, that it will be then that the judge decides whether to dismiss the case, or to permanently enforce the restraining order. He also advised me that he would be out of town on the date of the hearing, and that it would be wise of me to have an attorney present, because of the magnitude of the damage that could be done to the custody case had Tiffany convinced the judge to permanently enforce the restraining order.

So, I asked him if I should use Michael Anderson. He said Mr. Anderson would be fine for this court hearing. Michael is one of the attorneys that I had interviewed in January 2003 while I was still in a relationship with Tiffany. I chose not to hire him at that time because I was afraid of what would happen had I done so. As I left Mr. Peterson's office, I pulled out my phone, called Mr. Anderson and scheduled an appointment to see him. A day or two later I met with him and found out that I was going to have to pay him fifteen hundred dollars to have him represent me in this case to defend myself against a bogus restraining order.

In the restraining order, which is officially referred to as a domestic violence injunction, she stated that I was verbally abusing her at the hospital and that I had gotten in her face and threatened her. Now obviously none of this happened, as both of my parents were able to testify to, as well as one of the nurses at the hospital had testified to as well.

Before the hearing, I had gone to the hospital to get copies of the medical records so that I could prove that she brought our son to the hospital for no reason, other than to set me up. The medical reports proved that he wasn't sick at all. I believed that would be enough to prove that she was lying about our son's illness, which would destroy any credibility she would ever have. I was fortunate enough to find out that the nurse had noticed the irregular behavior of Tiffany and her mother and decided to write a full-page statement, sign it and attach it to our son's file, all on her own. In the statement she noted the irregular behavior and that the child wasn't even sick, and that there was no verbal or physical confrontation between us, other than the child's mother's irregular behavior, and that I had neither done nor said anything to contribute to a conflict. The fact that the nurse recognized what was happening, all on her own, and was wise enough to document it, and honest enough to do so, was a blessing.

I brought all the documents to court with me for the hearing. The court requires that each party and their attorney meet with a mediator separately, prior to going into the courtroom for the hearing. When we arrived at the courthouse, my attorney, Mr. Anderson and I sat down in a small room right outside the courtroom and the mediator began by advising us of what Tiffany had stated to him that she wanted, in order to resolve this domestic violence injunction hearing. He told us that Tiffany was demanding eight hundred dollars a month in child support. I was already paying two hundred and twenty dollars a month, from the date that she kidnapped him, all the way through the present time. I had absolutely no income at all and hadn't had any income in almost a year, as I had just started my business that hadn't been profitable yet.

Tiffany was also demanding to reduce the eight hours a week of "visitation" and the one overnight every other week that I had. Mr. Anderson basically laughed and told the mediator that child support and custody is a matter for the state court to handle, and that those issues have nothing to do with the domestic violence injunction hearing, which is held in the county court, and that if she wanted to try to use this bogus injunction to try to extort money out of his client that he would be more than happy to stand in front of the judge with her, and that he would, metaphorically speaking of course, "Chop her legs off at the knees".

I must admit that one of the things I loved about Michael Anderson was that while he was as calm at a kitten outside of the courtroom, he was as ferocious as a lion once he stepped into a courtroom.

Just before we stepped into the courtroom, a female representative from C.A.R.E, which is an acronym for The Center for Abuse & Rape Emergencies, was sitting down with Tiffany on the bench right outside the courtroom, instructing her on how to basically crucify the alleged male abuser in this case. They send volunteers to scour the halls of the courthouse searching for men that they can devour.

I'm sorry if the way in which I describe their intent is offensive to anyone reading this, but this woman was literally sitting there telling Tiffany exactly what lies to tell the judge in order to get the injunction to stick, with no regard for the truth. Now I'm sure that not all representatives of this organization act in such a malicious and unethical manner, but this one did.

A few moments later, we entered the courtroom, and the hearing began. Judge Williams presided over the case. Years later I would find out that Judge Williams was a Christian man and based upon all the feedback that I had received about him, he was an honest and reasonable judge. The judge begins by having each of us sworn in, promising to tell the whole truth, and nothing but the truth, so help you God. My attorney had the medical report and the statement from the hospital nurse and was ready to fight.

The judge read the injunction. It was filled with lies about me allegedly threatening her and verbally abusing her at the hospital, which the nurse's statement could prove to be false. I'm sure by this time she had obtained a copy of the hospital report, along with the nurse's signed statement and knew that she was screwed. After reading the injunction, the judge asked her if I had hit her. She didn't answer, so the judge asked again in a louder voice.

Knowing that the nurses report proved that she was already lying about everything else, and that the nurse had already stated that there was no physical conflict, she had no choice but to answer the judge's question honestly. She timidly said no. The judge then stated that a domestic violence injunction is only valid if the recipient of it physically struck the individual requesting the injunction. Because that didn't occur, he was going to dismiss this case.

The thing that irritated me is that while I basically won this case and the domestic violence injunction was thrown out, despite having evidence that her allegations she made under oath, under the penalty of perjury, were false, the court did nothing to reprimand her for filing a false domestic violence injunction. And on top of that, the judge that signed the temporary injunction, which wasn't Judge Williams, did so illegally.

The temporary domestic violence injunction order that the first judge had signed wasn't valid because it only included claims of verbal abuse and threats and didn't include an allegation of physical abuse. Not only did she get away with third degree felony perjury, but the judge that signed it did it illegally, with no consequences to him. The only price that was paid was by the innocent party, which was me, at a total cost of fifteen hundred dollars.

In addition to trying to gain an advantage in the custody case, she also did it in order to get rid of me during the exchanges for those two weeks so she could have access to my dad. During the exchanges for those two weeks, my mom told me that Tiffany and her mother were asking my dad to go over to their house, to tell him the "reason" why we ended our relationship.

They did this right in front of my mom and she wasn't happy about it. My mother told him that he shouldn't ever go over to their house to allow them to fill his head with lies. Now I honestly don't know what she thought she would've gained from filling his head with lies. But I do know that she chose him for this purpose because she knew he could be easily manipulated.

The one good thing that did come from the bogus restraining order was that her attorney, Mr. Smith, withdrew from the case because he was tired of the lies and malicious behavior of his client. Tiffany lost her free attorney as a result of filing a bogus restraining order. Mr. Smith filed a motion to withdraw from the case due to, "Irreconcilable differences on how to proceed with the case", as he stated on the court document. Throughout the thirteen and a half years of hell she put us through, this would not be the only attorney that dumped her because of her irrational and malicious behavior.

The next attorney she hired after losing Mr. Smith, Maria Thompson, told my attorney Todd Peterson at the end of the case, that she would never represent Tiffany ever again. Believe it or not, not all attorneys have the heartless, evil, money hungry character that the stereotype says they have. Some of them are very honest and are helpful advocates.

Chapter Thirteen

Laden with Happiness and Tears

Even though life was incredibly tough for me and my family, God gave us some beautiful times as well. I'd like to share them with you. When my son was about six months old, in June 2003, my sister and I had taken Jonathan to see my dad at work. My dad worked as a chef at a hospital. My sister and I walked into the cafeteria with Jonathan and we told the cashier that we were there to see my dad, Joseph Stone. My dad came out a few moments later and we all sat down at one of the tables in the cafeteria. My son was sipping on some apple juice while we visited.

My dad was holding him on his lap, bouncing him up and down and making googly noises to entertain him, when just a few moments later, we all begin to recognize this horrific smell. My dad picked him up off his lap, and we all were able to see that my dad's pants and shirt were all covered in poop. My son had diarrhea and it leaked out of the diaper and ended up all over my dad. My sister and I were laughing hysterically. We counted our time with Jonathan much more precious than most. Typical families just get to do life together, that was what we were the most grateful for, making forever memories with my beautiful baby boy. My dad was a great sport about it. Dad just went back to the locker room laughing. He kept an extra set of clothes in the locker room and he was able to take a quick shower and change before he went back to work.

Some of the other memories that I cherish from this time frame were the times I took him to a small amusement park in our hometown, called Kids World. It was right down the street from my house. They had a giant slide, a carousel, Ferris wheel, and many other rides designed for young children. We went there often.

We had so many enjoyable times there, what a blessing it was to see Jonathan's face light up with happiness. Watching my little boy laughing and squealing with delight meant the world to me. Kids World helped us forget about our troubles. My dad often joined us. Dad and my Jonathan shared such a special bond. It was a gift from God to see the bliss my family was having with carefree and lighthearted times together.

Dad and I took Jonathan out to eat often. I remember so fondly the first time he drank out of a straw. We were at a seafood restaurant and he was sitting in his high chair, probably around six to eight months old. We got him a glass of milk and we helped him hold the glass. He was able to drink out of a straw for the very first time. There were so many happy, "firsts". Each "first" that I got to witness, was a rare privilege to me. Later, when he was able to talk in full sentences, he would mention the name of his favorite food from each restaurant when we passed it. As we drove by McDonald's he would say, "French fries, French fries" in his cute little baby voice. When we drove by Denny's, he would say "eggies, eggies".

Everywhere we went people would go crazy over my little guy. He was so adorable and kind-hearted. Jonathan had thick black hair and angelic blue eyes. Grandparents and even young people would comment on his chubby cheeks and his sweet face or his incredibly thick black hair. Most babies, even at the age of one-year-old, don't have as much hair as he had when he was first born. During my "visits" with him, I would usually take him to places like the mall, where he would love to ride those motorized cars, trucks and planes. I loved the sound of his toddler voice, giggling with delight as he was taking off in his airplane. We had a lot of great times during the summer of 2003. I thank God it wasn't all chaos and suffering.

Now let's talk about some of the difficult things that we had to deal with during that summer. I remember my son coming home to me with soaking wet diapers that I could tell weren't changed for probably the entire morning and afternoon. Each time I picked him up, he was soaked, with a horrible rash as a result. Tiffany had clothes on him that didn't fit, they were too tight and filthy. He typically looked like he had not been bathed since the last time he was at my house, several days earlier. He would come home with the smell of smoke all over him. Tiffany was living with her mom and step dad after we separated and they both smoked cigarettes as well as other things. Tiffany's stepdad, George, was a drug dealer too, just like her biological dad. It was simply a horrible environment for a baby to be living in.

During this round of litigation, my attorney hired a private investigator to gather information for the case. He had taken photos of a vehicle that was frequently parked in the driveway of the house where Tiffany was living with our son. The P.I. ran the tags and found that the vehicle belonged to a well-known drug dealer in the community who had been arrested many times for possession with intent to distribute, and weapons charges.

As my son got a little older, I had to worry if he would get caught in the middle of a drug deal gone bad, or accidentally get into the guns that were in the house, or unknowingly get into the drugs.

George, Tiffany's stepdad, would frequently leave harassing and threatening messages on my voice mail, some of which I still have recorded on old answering machines that I have in the storage facility. Many times, in between the threats to rape and kill me, he would mention the pleasure he takes in using cocaine and heroin.

A few years later in 2008, he was shot and killed by another drug dealer that he owed a large sum of money to. Anyway, I knew my son was living in an environment where just about anything you could imagine could happen.

There was also a time when he was a bit older, around three or four. My sister had gone grocery shopping for me during tax season one time and brought my son with her. When I got home from work, I asked my sister for the bag of sugar she had picked up from the store. My son said, "I know where it is". He walked over to the cabinet and grabbed the bag of sugar to hand to me, when he blurted out, "Mommy puts sugar up her nose". My sister and I simply looked at each other, absolutely stunned.

We didn't ask him to elaborate. I suppose it was because I didn't want to unintentionally drag him into the middle of the chaos that his mom created. By that time, I also knew there was nothing I could do about it anyway. My theory is that he probably woke up in the middle of the night and walked out into the living room to find his mom. When he saw her snorting cocaine, and asked her what it was, she probably told him it was just sugar.

Chapter Fourteen
Lies, Lies, and More Lies

As the summer of 2003 passed, the bogus restraining had come and gone, we began to move into doing the depositions. I believe we deposed Tiffany first. I only remember some of the highlights of the deposition, which included her lying under oath and committing several counts of perjury. I don't remember all the details, but I do remember my attorney acting like a Harvard educated pit bull. He questioned her about the reasoning for denying me contact with my son for sixty-six days and nights.

Tiffany's story was that she was afraid that I would kidnap him and leave the state. The irony with this story is that she was actually the one that kidnapped him. It is a common symptom of a person with Borderline Personality Disorder to project their own qualities, characteristics, and traits on to the opposing party. They accuse you of what they are doing.

Todd Peterson said to her, "So you mean to tell me Tiffany, that you honestly believe that a man that had just bought a home, started a business, and whose entire family lives right here in Florida, was going to leave all of that behind and take his son and leave the state?" She said "Yes".

She also alleged when she was pregnant that I threatened to kill her if she ever took my son away from me. My attorney caught the fact that she specified son and he knew she was lying. He proceeded to ask her when this alleged threat had taken place. She told him that it was in May, just a couple of weeks after finding out she was pregnant. He then asked other questions that weren't related to that topic, then after a few minutes he came back to questions pertaining to the alleged threat. He asked her about her gynecologist, what his name was, how often she had to go for checkups, and if I attended the doctor's visits with her.

He then asked her when she and I found out about the gender of the baby. She told him it was in August 2002, when we had the first ultrasound. He then asked her, "You told me several minutes ago that in May 2002 Mr. Stone threatened to kill you if you took his son from him. How is it possible that in May 2002 he threatened you kill you if you took away his son, when you just stated to me that neither of you knew the gender of the baby until August 2002?" Her answer was something to the effect of, "Oops, I must have misspoken, I didn't mean to say son, I meant to say child". He did a great job of catching her on every lie. He acknowledged to me that no one would ever care that she committed several counts of perjury, but at least her credibility had dropped down to zero. At least it would help me defend myself against any other lies that she would come up with. Overall the deposition was a success. We had won that battle, and by then, she realized that she was losing the war.

The fact that my son was in a drug, and chain-smoking environment broke my heart. He was clearly abused by his mother and grandmother and treated as an unwanted pain in the rear end. The only reason Tiffany fought so hard to have custody of our son was so she could keep getting checks and also because she knew how torn up and inconsolable I was because of the abuse. Honestly, I felt like each time I lost in a hearing, or had restricted custody, she got a sick thrill out of it.

Now because she was female, if she had been a good mother and a mentally stable woman, she would have been able to secure full custody for herself, with me maintaining only hours a week of visitation. The court was now aware of the kidnapping, bogus restraining order, harassment, and all of the screaming and violence that occurred every time we exchanged our son. My lawyer did a great job in bringing out the constant lying in the deposition. He also was able to bring out all the other crazy things she did. Tiffany was facing a moderate to high chance of at least a fifty-fifty time share arrangement being ordered by the court. She wasn't content with this.

Tiffany wanted to destroy the man that in her mind, had rejected and abandoned her. Tiffany's severely damaged mind couldn't bear the pain, and accept the fact that she was indeed a broken mess, in need of fixing.

The fixing she needed could not be done with medication. No psychiatrist in the world could ever heal her. She was and still is in desperate need of help, help that only God can give her. For years, my son and I would pray for her every night, praying for her healing. And even to this day, I continue to pray for her and for her recovery. (Matthew 5:44)

In December 2003, nine months after we separated and about eight months into the litigation, it was time for Tiffany and her attorney to take my deposition. By this time, her second attorney, Maria Thompson, had become irritated with her client and the two of them had a significant difference of opinion on how to proceed. Just like Tiffany's first attorney, Maria Thompson wasn't happy with her lying, cheating and her insatiable thirst for pain and destruction. Tiffany even chose not to attend my deposition because she was so angry at Maria for disagreeing with her. Maria, however, did the job she was hired to do. We did a two to three-hour deposition. The primary goal her client assigned to her was to acquire money. She did not care what was in the best interest of our son, she just wanted more money. So, the majority of the deposition was about my tax preparation franchise. Very little of it had anything to do with our son.

She asked, "How much revenue did the business earn in 2003? How much was spent on rent? How much was spent on payroll? How much were all the other expenses?" Even though I stated that the company had made no money in its first year, Maria spent two hours doing forensic accounting, requesting every figure from every line of the company's profit-and-loss statement. I had nothing to hide, so I gave her all the info she requested. I believe she was aware of the fact that there was no money made, and there was no money to be stolen.

Some of the questions had been focused on the lies that Tiffany had told her about how I was allegedly verbally abusive to her, when in fact the truth was that those accusations were nothing more than the behavioral pattern known as projection. Projection is what people with BPD do to place their own painful and shameful characteristics on someone else, so that way they don't have to face the ugly truth that they see every time they look in the mirror.

Maria asked me about a time that according to Tiffany, I had allegedly punched the bathroom door, cracking it. After laughing, and after Mr. Peterson kicked my leg under the table for laughing when it was probably not in my best interest to do so, I told her that while that never happened, I would be more than happy to tell her about the hole that Tiffany punched into the living room wall that my dad had to fix.

I was also very happy to tell her about the holes she broke in the wall of the bedroom when she threw her keys, that my dad also patched up. When it was all done, I had more ammunition to take to the judge with me. Her attorney's entire deposition of me revolved around my company and what money she could try to steal from me. It had very little to do with our son. By the grace of God, at the end of the day, we survived.

Chapter Fifteen

Trial

On Monday, January 6, 2004, we were at the courthouse preparing for the beginning of the trial. To make things even more complicated, just a few days earlier we found out that Judge Peter Jones was moved to a different courthouse. We now had another judge, named Robert Nelson, that no one knew anything about. My attorney had no experience handling a trial in this judge's courtroom. We had at least two other hearings with our former judge, and he saw what was happening.

We now were walking blindly into this trial, in front of a new judge, with no idea of which way our case would go. We didn't know if this judge was abused by his father or if he had a bad divorce himself or whatever other crazy baggage he carried with him. We simply lost the security we had just gained with the former judge, because he finally saw the truth about Tiffany's insanity and cruelty.

My attorney and I, and my mom and dad were already in the courtroom when Tiffany and her attorney walked in. The bailiff then instructed us all to stand while the judge walked into the courtroom. Before we got started, Maria advised the judge that she would like to talk to attorney Todd Peterson to discuss a possible settlement prior to beginning the trial. The judge granted her request, allowing us 15 minutes before we had to return.

We each went outside of the courtroom into two separate rooms while our attorneys had a brief discussion in the hallway. Mr. Peterson came into the room a few moments later and advised me that they are offering a deal where I would have 2.5 days a week with my son, with me paying $220 a month in child support. Also, Tiffany would need to be designated primary residential parent, which would've meant that she would be given all the decision-making capabilities.

I respectfully declined the offer, with one of my primary concerns being the designation of primary residential parent being given to her. There was no way I would agree to that. I would have taken my chances with the judge if that was the only other option. Mr. Peterson said, "If we agreed on a designation of co-primary residential parents, would you be willing to consider that?". I told him I could at least sit down and think about it at that point. He went and talked to Maria Thompson and came back and told me that they would agree to that.

I was now placed in a position where I would have to make a decision that would not only affect quite possibly the rest of my life, but also my son's life. It was a burden that I don't believe anyone should have to bear. I asked Mr. Peterson what he thought I should do. He refused to give me an opinion, but rather chose to describe to me the possible outcomes of a trial. He did state that the court always rules in the favor of the mother. If the judge chose not to care about all the things that Tiffany did wrong, he could order the standard deal for dads, which was a couple of hours twice a week and one overnight every week. Or, if the judge was moved by the damage that Tiffany had done, he might possibly lean towards a 50/50 split, at best.

No matter what, Peterson's opinion was that there was no way that justice would be served, and no way the judge would ever take a child away from a mother, no matter how bad she is. With the spectrum going from a few hours, twice a week with one overnight per week, to 3.5 days a week at best, I decided that 2.5 days was the best decision I could make for my son.

I figured that guaranteeing him 2.5 days a week of peace, safety and security, and taking him away from the violence and abuse for those 2.5 days a week, would be better than the worst-case scenario. I made the toughest decision of my life at that time and I agreed to the 2.5 days a week. I didn't like it, and it wasn't fair, but I figured it would be best to walk away and come back to fight another day. Besides, I knew that I had the promise of God to look forward to and that He would someday bring my baby home. I chose to leave it in His hands and trust Him.

Chapter Sixteen

Child Abuse

Any reasonable person would assume that after all of this fighting, that this would be over, and everybody would just move on. That wasn't the case with Tiffany. She never moves on. When you become the object of a BPD's obsession, it's like a life sentence, with no chance of parole. There is no where you can run and no where you can hide that will ever make you safe from this person. It was a life sentence for a crime that I never committed. A life sentence, simply for loving my son, and wanting to be his father. A life sentence that is questionably worse than being behind bars.

I faced more than a decade of lies, false accusations, harassment, threats, vandalism, stalking, child abuse, and even attempted murder. While all of this was bad enough, it could in some way be forgivable and forgettable, considering that as the saying goes, all is fair in love and war. While this was never my philosophy, I can see how any ruthless person would probably stoop to the same level that she did during the first legal battle. However, by this point, enough should have been enough. How could I know it was just the beginning? It was only after the court settlement on January 6, 2004 that the games really began.

It was only a few days later, on January 9, 2004, that the unthinkable happened. While she was always violent natured, meaning, she would yell, scream, throw things, and raise her fist as she threatened to hit me, she never actually did hit me. As I'm sure I mentioned before, the only reason that she never actually hit me was due to her awareness of the fact that I would defend myself.

I was always under constant threat of physical abuse while in the relationship with her. While I had known that she was violent natured, I never wanted to believe that she would ever do anything to physically hurt our son. And while I tried hard not to believe that it was possible, I would soon find out I was wrong.

One morning in January, just days after our court settlement, my mom and I went to pick up my son from her at Eckerd's, which was the designated exchange location at the time. After leaving the parking lot, we headed to the grocery store to purchase some things. When we were in the store, we noticed that my son had a severe burn on the palm of his hand. We were shocked. Tiffany never mentioned it at the drop off, so I of course wanted to know what had happened.

The burn was so severe, that it had blistered, and the blisters were starting to peel, or fall off. I don't remember exactly how it looked, other than to describe it as "the flesh was hanging off of his hand". I was so shocked and upset. I immediately called Tiffany to ask her what had happened. She didn't answer the phone of course. Tiffany would later send me an email with a story of how it allegedly happened. She hadn't taken him to a doctor or hospital for treatment. She had stated in an email that she didn't feel as though it was significant enough to need medical attention. Because she did not answer the phone or return my call, and I didn't read her email until later that night, I had no choice but to seek medical attention for him.

It was a Friday afternoon and his pediatrician's office was closed, so my mom and I took him to the hospital to have the burn checked out. It looked like it was a day or two old at this time. After waiting an hour or two, we were finally taken back to see a doctor. He looked at it and gave us some prescription strength cream to use a couple of times a day for a week, in order to speed up and enhance the healing process and wrapped his hand up in a bandage. He instructed us to change the bandage once or twice a day.

The doctor was also surprised at the burn, asked how it happened and I told him I didn't know, and that I picked him up from his mother like this. I know doctors are required by law to report suspected abuse, but he never did. I know how busy doctors in a hospital setting can be but reporting abuse can save a child's life. Perhaps if the doctor had, Jonathan would have been returned to me earlier.

Now later on when I got home and read Tiffany's email, she described the story on how it supposedly happened. According to her, our son was walking through the living room at her mom's house, where she was living with our son at the time. He reached out his hand and touched a light bulb on a lamp that didn't have a lampshade on it. Apparently, our thirteen-month-old son placed his hand on a light bulb, and after feeling the heat and pain instantaneously, he decided to hold his hand on it long enough to sustain a second-degree burn.

Jonathan must have decided, at thirteen months old, to hold his hand on the light bulb for a minute or two, in order to sustain a second-degree burn. Now, while it is true that I wasn't there at the time it happened, and I am not a doctor, I can tell you that I tested the theory myself by placing my hand on a 100-watt light bulb for an extended period of time.

I don't remember how long because this was many years ago, but I had to make the conscious decision to place my hand on the light bulb and hold it there for an extended period of time. It was at least one full minute. Typically, if a person had accidentally placed their hand on a light bulb, it would take only one second to realize that it hurt and to react by removing your hand from the light bulb.

I held my hand on it for sixty seconds or more, and while it hurt like crazy, it did not cause a second-degree burn. It did not blister. The skin on my hand didn't fall off. What it did do, was turn my hand red, and then it hurt for quite a while. I ran cold water over it for several minutes to dull the pain and when it was all said and done, there was no blistering, no bruising, no permanent damage done.

After a few hours the redness disappeared, and the discomfort had gone away. I didn't suffer any kind of burn, not even a lesser first-degree burn. So, while this still doesn't prove that she did anything wrong, there is one more piece of information that Tiffany had shared with me in that email that I must tell you before you form your own opinion on the matter.

Not only did she tell me that our son had been walking through the living room when he had placed his hand on the light bulb, but she also told me that when our son had touched the light bulb, it wasn't even turned on! That's right, according to her, our son sustained a second-degree burn, with the flesh falling off of his hand, by touching a light bulb, but not just any old light bulb, it was a light bulb that wasn't even turned on at the time he touched it.

Now this is the story that was presented to me in writing. I don't have to be a doctor, nor did I have to be there to witness it, in order to know that it is impossible to sustain a second-degree burn from touching a light bulb that isn't even turned on. At this point, I was very concerned for the safety of my son. I called my attorney and explained everything to him and he advised me to be cautious in regard to making any abuse reports with child protective services.

Basically, he told me to keep my mouth shut because the authorities wouldn't do anything about it anyway. And if I did report it, that would make me look like a crying, over reacting dad who was trying to cause trouble. Really? Is this really what our child protective services is really like? I honestly would never believe that to be true, at least not until I had seen it for myself. I took my attorneys advice and didn't ask any more questions. I had to shut up and look the other way. In essence, this is how it would be for the next ten plus years.

In addition to the burn on his hand, my mom and I had also discovered on that same day that one of my son's ears was severely black and blue. This, combined with all the other facts, led me to formulate the opinion that she must have willfully placed his hand onto the burner on a stove, and while doing so, he jerked to the side, while in severe pain, and hit the side of his head on the stove, leaving him with his ear severely bruised. Having to visualize this in my mind, is making me feel the pain that my son went through at that moment. No parent should have to watch their child suffer like this.

There would be one more time that the topic of my son sustaining a second-degree burn on his hand would come up. It was in August 2004, we had already found our way back to the courtroom for round two, and I decided that I would question Tiffany about it while she was under oath.

This time, she explained that she was carrying our son in her arms when he reached his hand out and touched a light bulb that wasn't turned on and sustained a second-degree burn. After she explained this to the judge, I simply held up a copy of the email that she had sent me in January right after the burn, and I asked her why she stated several months earlier in her email to me that our son was walking when he touched the light bulb and now, she is telling me that she was carrying him. I asked her, which one was it? It can't be both. It is possible that one is true, and one is a lie. Or, could it be that both contradicting versions of the same story are both lies. Which one is it?

Tiffany couldn't answer. All she did, is start crying. Whether it was an attempt to gain sympathy from the judge, or whether she had actually felt shame for what she had done, I'm not sure. The judge never required her to answer the question and simply moved on to the next topic.

After my son sustained the burn on his hand, his behavior changed significantly. He was only thirteen months old and couldn't talk. He was walking at that time but didn't say much more than daddy and momma. The very next day after I picked Jonathan up from his mom with the burn on his hand, I dropped him back off to her. He cried and screamed as hot tears poured down his little face. He was scared to death. When I picked him up out of his car seat and he saw his own mother, he put his head down on my shoulder and started crying hysterically, wrapping his small toddler arms tightly around me with a death grip. He was holding on for dear life and he didn't want to go to Tiffany. It made me so sad to see this, but I had no choice.

I was forced to return my son to the person that was abusing him. No choice at all. I was helpless. When I tried to hand him to his mother, he wouldn't let go of me. He wrapped his arms around me with the strength of a bear. It was tearing me up inside, just like it is now, as I'm writing this. I knew this wouldn't be easy, having to relive all of this in my mind as the memories are like hot daggers in my heart.

Once again, the keyboard of my computer, is soaked with the tears of pain. Reliving this is the last thing I want to do. It doesn't make sense to choose to relive the memories of handing my baby over to a person that had just burned his hand on a stove, on purpose, because she was angry at the outcome of the court settlement just a few days earlier. I had survived, and she wasn't happy about that. I'm asking myself right now, why am I doing this? As I pause and think, I realize that this is for a greater purpose. A purpose much greater than myself.

She ended up forcefully grabbing him out of my arms. As she held him up in her hands, he was screaming, like the scream you hear in a horror film, when the killer is holding the knife in front of the woman's face, just about to kill her. My little boy started swinging his arms, hitting her repeatedly on her shoulders, desperately trying to escape.

I turned around and walked to my car, my eyes filling with tears. I couldn't watch any more. I had to walk away and leave my son with Tiffany. Can you fathom, your baby is in your arms, holding on to you with a bear hug, crying endless tears, so terrified and not able to tell you what was wrong and why he was so afraid? I, as his father could do nothing to ease his fear. I had to watch as the terror consumed him and there was nothing I could do to protect my baby.

What could I do? I was required by law to do this. The law said I had to hand my innocent, defenseless child over to a person that had just purposefully and severely abused him. The law said I had to walk away. What kind of law is this? What kind of law would not only do this to a child, but what kind of law would force a parent to be complicit with such a horrendous atrocity?

This heartbreaking sad scene would play itself out over and over again. Each and every time I would have to drop him off in the parking lot of Eckerd Drugs, Jonathan would scream in fear and cry and whimper, wishing he could stay with me. This went on for several months until the trauma had worn off. There was one time in March 2004, just two months after his mom burned him, I was driving with him to one of my tax offices.

While we were on the way to my office, we passed by another Eckerd Drug store location, approximately 50 miles away from home. When he saw the building, he burst into tears, screaming in a panic, afraid that I was going to drop him off to his mother. I pulled to the side of the road and grabbed a tissue to wipe the tears that were streaming down his face. It took me several minutes to calm him down and assure him that he wasn't going back to his mother that day.

It was like he was suffering from post-traumatic stress disorder. Another time, when he was just a little older and could talk, we went to Eckerd Drugs to drop him off. We got there a few minutes early, so we parked the car in the parking lot and waited for his mother to arrive. A few minutes later, he saw her car at the stoplight across the street, as she was on her way over. When he saw her car, he started yelling, "There's mommy. She's coming, she's coming! Please daddy, please, hurry, start the car, let's go. Let's leave!"

The exchanges were always filled with chaos. Tiffany would get out of the car yelling and screaming, and sometimes throwing things at us. It became a regular thing for my son to come home to me with cuts and bruises, always with either no explanation, or with some ridiculous story attached.

For those of you that have experienced abuse growing up, I want you to understand that I do sincerely believe that God has a purpose and a plan for the pain. I know some of you are reading this and relating to the pain and frustration of a child being hurt, because you or someone you care about went through this as a child. So many of you will ask, "Why would God allow this? There can't be a God, because if there was, He certainly wouldn't let this happen".

We must remember that we live in a world that was designed to be perfect, but because Adam and Eve allowed sin to come into the world, we now live in a world that is broken. A world that is driven by the free will of man, rather than by the will of God. A free will that unfortunately is frequently used for evil rather than for good.

People choose to do the things they do. It is not God that forces them to do what they do, nor does God condone the evil things that people do. You can read the entire Bible from cover to cover and see that it is not His will that evil would happen. It is His will that we turn the other cheek. It is His will that we forgive. It is His will that we do unto others as we would have them do unto us.

It is our will, the will of man, that creates war, that inspires hate, that initiates murder, that contrives rape. It is our will that creates the sin that happens in this world. Could God stop these things? Sure, of course He could, He is GOD. Then why doesn't He? For Him to stop these things, He would have to take away our free will. He would have to take away our ability to choose, our ability to live as He created us to, in His Image.

The Bible says we were created in His image, with a soul, with a free will and the ability to choose to love one another, like He does, or we can choose to hate and live in a different kingdom than the one that God does. When we choose to hate, we will live in darkness where Satan and all his cohorts live.

Chapter Seventeen
How Do I Get Out of This Nightmare?

In April 2004, just about four months after we finalized the court settlement, we were back in court again. I had to file a motion for contempt because Tiffany was refusing to abide by the court's custody agreement. She was refusing to share holidays, coming up with excuses for why she couldn't drop him off to me. I don't remember everything that went on, but what I do remember is that we both chose to represent ourselves during this series of court proceedings.

We met for mediation prior to any court hearings, as was required by the court. We managed to agree on resolutions for about half of the issues at hand. With the other half of the issues still unresolved, we ended up continuing the case and going to court several times throughout the summer and fall of 2004. One thing I need to point out about the day of mediation, is that Tiffany had her mother there. I don't remember all the details of the heated discussions. What I do remember is that when I was in the hallway of the courthouse, Tiffany's mother came up to me and was getting in my face, spewing out lies, harassment and all the usual garbage.

One other thing I remember her saying was that the next time I picked up my son, he would have a bruise on his face. I don't know why she would threaten to hurt him but hurting him had become a regular occurrence. I told the court employee that was working with us as our mediator that my son's grandmother had just threatened to hurt him. I thought I should document the threat in some way, shape or form, so that if it happened, someone else would already be aware of.

The very next day I received a call from a lady named Barbara Gonzalez from the Florida Department of Children and Family Services. She told me she had received a report that my son was not being bathed when he was with me. That he lived in a dirty house and wasn't being cared for properly. She said the report stated that I was leaving him in dirty diapers all day and was basically being negligent.

Amazingly, Tiffany accused me of doing everything she had been doing and filed a false report with DCFS. I remember telling Barbara that I wouldn't be picking up my son until the next morning, so she agreed to come and visit the next day when my son was there. The next morning, I picked my son up from his mother, and sure enough, there was a huge bruise on his cheek.

I would always take photos of all the burns, bruises and cuts throughout the years, just to document everything of significance that happened. My attorney taught me to take notes, photos, and create a paper trail of everything. I'm sure I didn't understand why at the time, but I just did what he told me to do. I still have the photo of this bruise in a storage facility with about eight file-sized boxes of legal documents. There would end up being a total of five times we reopened this case to play the sick games that Tiffany was enjoying so much.

When Barbara came over later that afternoon, she saw that my home was a brand new 2,012 square foot home that I just had built and moved into in March of 2004. I had all brand-new furniture, and being a neat freak my whole life, the house was always clean. My boy was in bed sleeping when she came over. I showed her the bruise on his face and told her that his grandmother had threatened to hurt him just a couple of days earlier while we were at mediation. I even gave her the name of the mediator, the lady that I told about the grandmother's threat. I'm not sure if she investigated it, probably not, because Barbara ended up closing the case, with no findings of evidence to support the allegations that Tiffany had made.

It was sad that Tiffany would start filing false DCFS reports, with false allegations of neglect and abuse. This would be the first of many false DCFS reports and false police reports that she would file throughout the years. I would spend the next 12 years of my life dealing with false accusations and the threat of false accusations. Constantly having to live my life looking over my shoulder, wondering if today would be the day that the police knock on my door to arrest me for false accusations of child abuse, or child molestation.

I had to spend the next twelve years of my life walking on eggshells, afraid to awaken the beast. I was extremely careful not to rock the boat too much, often having to look the other way when Tiffany would continue to play her sick little games, like violating a court order. I gave in to her demands for more money, and for anything else she wanted. If I didn't surrender, I would either be in prison right now for crimes I didn't commit, or Tiffany would have continued to hurt my son, worse than she did before. I did everything I could to keep the peace, which was almost impossible. Tiffany couldn't live in peace. Her mind was in ruins, constantly going and creating chaos. Tiffany had to externalize that chaos and create it when there wasn't any.

We would proceed to court to address the unresolved contempt of court issues. Our court ordered custody agreement had specifically stated that both parties were to consult with each other and make all decisions regarding our son's health, welfare and education jointly. Tiffany simply refused to do this. One of the issues that needed to be addressed at the first hearing for the contempt of court lawsuit was the fact that after getting our son's first pediatrician to drop us as clients, because she refused to follow any of the doctor's orders, she chose another pediatrician without discussing it with me and refused to even tell me what doctor she had chosen.

When this was presented to the judge, he then ordered Tiffany to disclose to me the name and address of the doctor she had chosen. However, he stated that her selection, despite being made in violation of the law, would remain, and of course, there would be no consequences for her violating the law. The second issue was her unilateral selection of a day care facility without discussing it with me and refusing to inform me of the name and location of the daycare that our son would be at three days a week.

Again, this was done in violation of the law, and again, the judge simply ordered her to disclose the name and location to me, and again, would not deem it necessary to allow me to have any input on the selection of the daycare that my son attended, despite the fact that the written law had required me to have that right.

It was in the first hearing that she was ordered to release that information to me, and after that first hearing I was finally able to visit the daycare facility and do an inspection of it. What I found wasn't great. I found out that the daycare, Kid Kingdom, had numerous violations on record with the Department of Children and Family services and had also been fined on numerous occasions.

When I had brought my concerns to the judge during the second hearing, I had first suggested that because of the daycare's less that flattering history, I should be allowed to consult with

Tiffany, as our court order required, to find a daycare that would be better for our son. His response was, "The daycare that your son is in now is licensed, therefore he will stay in that one."

How in the world does a judge ignore the fact that the court ordered judgment has been broken? The judge was refusing to enforce it, refusing to impose penalties for the violation of the law, he also went so far as to ignore the fact that the daycare wasn't an adequate choice for anyone's child, based on document-able violations and fines that the daycare had incurred.

This flagrant disregard for the law and this arrogant disregard for the child's best interest should have been enough for this judge to be taken away in handcuffs. It would only be a few years after this that the Kid Kingdom daycare would end up being closed by the state of Florida's Department of Children and Family Services. When the judge refused to allow me to have my court ordered input on the selection of my son's daycare, I then requested, after explaining to the judge that I'm self-employed and can stay home and take care of my son while his mother was working, to avoid the need and expense of daycare, to allow me to take care of my son while Tiffany was working. His response was "Mr. Stone, you already have more time with your child than most men do, therefore, I will not grant your request."

I wasn't allowed to take care of my son because of my gender. The judge thought that a minimum wage sixteen-year-old employee of Kid Kingdom would be able to care for our son better than the child's own parent. And the reason for this, was simply because of that parent's gender.

In addition to her violations of the court order, we had to address several false accusations that Tiffany had made alleging that I was violating the court order as well. It wasn't enough for her that she would continue to create pandemonium by refusing to obey the custody agreement, Tiffany had to get even by attacking me with a counter petition listing several made up violations of the court ordered custody agreement concerning me.

I don't remember them all of them, but I do remember one of the allegations. I was ordered to pay Tiffany two hundred and twenty dollars a month for "child support", earlier in the year. I started to make payments quarterly. I made the payments to her three months in advance. I did this because it was more convenient for me. Rather than mailing a check every month, and risking the possibility of forgetting one time, especially during the months of January through April, when I was working around the clock during tax season, I felt that any parent would be grateful to be paid several months early, rather than the clear majority of parents that make child support payments late, or not at all.

However, this would be twisted against me and Tiffany would complain to the court that I was in contempt because I was paying her three months in advance, rather than once a month, and somehow, this was a burden to her. The court Magistrate, Paul Alexander, had found me to be in contempt of court for not only paying my child support on time, but paying it early and paying it in advance.

When I asked him to explain to me how paying on time, early, and in advance could constitute contempt and where in the court order did it specify that I had to make payments in any specific interval, he couldn't answer, and I think he got angry that I had questioned his authority. That was another mistake. We were on one crazy merry-go-round, and it seemed the more I questioned how to make things flow peacefully so that we could avoid the trappings of the legal system, the worse it became!

This would be one of the many things that would make a mockery of the Florida court system. Not only was it common practice for the courts to automatically take children away from their dads for no reason, they would also do anything they could to further demonize fathers. The legal system would stop just short of making the false accusations themselves. They would wait for the parent to make the false accusations, and then simply go along with it.

This second round of litigation kept us occupied through the fall of 2004, and ended just months before the next round of chaos would begin. The next round would not be fought in a courtroom, where the rewards or consequences were written on a piece of paper. Instead, this next round was fought outside of the courtroom, outside the realm of the law, where lives were literally at stake, specifically, mine.

Chapter Eighteen

Co-Conspirators

In the summer of 2003, shortly after ending my relationship with Tiffany, I started dating a young woman that had worked for me earlier in the year. Jessica was a young, attractive, and intelligent girl, and quite the player. She had assumed that because I owned a business, that I had to have a lot of money. I discovered she was not interested in me, but interested in her next payday. You see, she was one of those women that, rather than working for a living, would spend her life pursuing other people's money.

Jessica enjoyed dating men of wealth, like doctors, lawyers, and business owners. She would use her beauty to lure foolish and ignorant men into relationships, just so she could manipulate them into spending tons of money on her. The only problem she had when she met me was that I wasn't as naive as the other guys she dated, nor was I as foolish as I was just a year or two earlier. I never spent money on her, nothing more than dinner and a movie. She was accustomed to men buying her jewelry, cars and vacations. One time she said to me, "Most guys buy me fur coats, jewelry, take me on expensive trips and take me to fancy restaurants. All you take me to is Arby's". And I said, with a smile on my face, "Yup, that's right. I'm smarter than those other guys." Anyway, shortly after we started dating, she realized that I had no money and decided we should just be friends.

In the spring of 2004 she needed a place to stay, so I let her live at my house for a couple of months. Jessica had a daughter around the same age as my son, so they would end up playing together on weekends, when my son was at home with me. Occasionally Jessica would babysit my son for me when I needed her to. It wasn't very often. I only had Jonathan 2.5 days a week, so I was very reluctant to leave him with anyone because I wanted to spend as much time with him as possible.

Since I was self-employed, I was able to work my schedule around his life, so I could take care of him the 2.5 days a week he was with me. I still managed to run a business with six offices in four different cities, working 80 hours a week, on the days that he was with his mother. I always made sure he received all of my time, and my complete attention when he was with me. That kind of schedule was easier when I was younger and healthier. Presently, I don't think I could do all that.

During the time that Jessica was staying at my house, Tiffany and I were busy in court. In June 2004, my friend Daniel came to spend the summer at my house while he was on his summer break from college. This would become a tradition for the next several years. He was a student at a college in northern Florida and would spend the summers at my house.

As Daniel was moving in, Jessica was moving out. She didn't want to stay there with another person that she didn't know. She was upset that I was allowing Daniel to move in, hoping that I would decide to not let him move in so that she could stay. I never kicked her out of the house. I told her she could still stay. I had two extra bedrooms, one for her and one for Daniel. She wasn't interested in staying if I had Daniel moving in. She decided to move out, and she wasn't happy about it.

I later found out that she had an outstanding warrant. I think it was for failure to appear in court. I'm guessing she wasn't comfortable having someone that she didn't know very well living there because she was probably afraid that he could potentially turn her in. The day she packed up her stuff to move, I was out and about somewhere, I don't remember where. But when I came home, she was gone.

I received a call from American Express's fraud department asking me if I was in Altamonte Springs using my card at a paint store. I told them I was at home and hadn't used the card at all that day. After listing several fraudulent charges that were made on the card, they closed the account and ordered a new card for me. I didn't confront her about it, I had too much going on. I suppose that I just assumed that if I'm not liable for it, I would leave it alone, and never let her in my house again, I thought I could just forget about it.

It wasn't until December 2004 that I had mentioned it to her during a conversation. I don't remember why I did, and I remember telling her that I didn't care, and that it wasn't a big deal, but she became very angry that I mentioned it. Of course, she denied it. I'd have to assume she was afraid I would turn her in to the police for theft, because from that time forward, we were no longer friends.

It wasn't until after this time that I became curious about this girl's past, so I went to the clerk of the courts office and did a background check on her and her brothers. There were, of course, many arrests made for DUI's, grand theft, drugs, etc. The most interesting arrest was for Jessica. Just a couple years earlier she was arrested for assault with a deadly weapon. Apparently, she tried to run over her ex-boyfriend with her car in the parking lot of the mall.

One of the lessons I learned from these experiences was that you should always do background checks on any significant others that you are considering as a potential candidate for a relationship. It's amazing how much you can find out about a person with a simple background check. With all the social media that's available today, you can easily find out a lot about a person and possibly save yourself a lot of misery, just by doing your homework and making educated decisions.

It wasn't until a couple of months later that she would pop up again in my life. My son was almost two-and-a-half years old, when we were at my parents' house one evening and I was walking with him as he rode his little power wheels motorcycle, when he stopped for a moment, he blurted out, "Mommy took me to see Diana". Diana was Jessica's daughter. At this point in time, I hadn't seen or associated myself with Jessica for several months. It was interesting to hear my son say that his mom had taken him to see Jessica's daughter, obviously meaning that she had met with Jessica.

He didn't tell me anymore than that, and I was always careful not to ask him too many questions because I didn't want to ever drag him in the middle of any problems that his mother and I had. But this revelation would begin what was one of the most interesting years in this story

Chapter Nineteen
Mafia Messages

After Jessica and I had our falling out over the stolen credit card, it became obvious, through my son telling me that his mom had met with her, that they were going to be working together to plan something that would certainly be to my detriment. As the next several months passed, things would begin to get a little crazy.

One morning my son and I went to have breakfast with my mom and dad. It was at a great family owned and operated restaurant called Antonio's, right up the street from my parents' home. We had just ordered our breakfast, when a young man, probably in his early twenties, sat down at a small table right next to us. He began to politely make conversation with us, and as he did so, my mom asked if he was by himself.

He said he was waiting to meet someone there. As we were all talking, he asked me about my son and I told him he was two years old. He then asked where we were from and we told him Massachusetts. I figured he could recognize my mother's Boston accent. We asked him where he was from, and he said he was from Milwaukee.

I can't speak for my mom and dad, but I knew I felt that the excessive friendliness and inquisitiveness of this young man, by himself, was a little odd. Sure enough, it was just a few moments later in the conversation that he said something that raised another red flag warning. During the casual conversation he once again commented on where he was from. Rather than the hometown of Milwaukee that he mentioned earlier, this time he said that he was from Michigan.

It was then that it all came together that indeed something wasn't right. He had slipped up and had made a mistake. I'm not sure if he realized it or not, but I did. He had stated earlier that he was from Milwaukee, which is in Wisconsin, not Michigan. Michigan however, is where Jessica was born and raised.

I realized what was going on, so I told my parents to watch my son because I had to go get something that I had forgotten out of my car. I wanted to go outside to see if there was anyone else there, or if my car had been vandalized or the tires flattened. There didn't appear to be anything out of the ordinary happening outside. I came back in and sat down.

Moments later, he got up and said he had to go to the bathroom. He walked right out the front door, probably realizing that I had figured out what he was really doing there. What was very concerning to us was the fact that they had apparently been stalking us for quite a while, for them to know exactly where we were. I'm not sure if his slip of the tongue was intentional, to let me know who he was and why he was there. Or, if it was an accident, and he was there just to get a closer look at us, or to try to find out some information from us. I'm not sure what his intent was that day, but I would soon realize that these two severely mentally ill women were serious about trying to cause some problems.

It was only a few days later that I had walked out of a department store to get inside my 2005 Dodge Dakota pickup truck, to find a five-inch nail jabbed into the side of my front passenger side tire. It was easy to see who had done this. I had to go get my tire fixed, to find out that it would cost $135 to replace it.

This was only the beginning, as Tiffany and Jessica ramped up their efforts to hurt me. It didn't take long to notice a pattern that would develop with the tire slashing, the stalking, and all the rest of the bedlam. It always happened on the days and nights that my son wasn't home with me. All the attacks happened when he was at his mother's home. This pattern had been one of many clues that would make it obvious who was behind it all. Not to mention the fact that while I was driving home one evening, I noticed a white car sitting on an empty lot just a few hundred feet before my house. When I noticed this, I slowed down as I passed so I could look at the driver. As I slowly passed by, I turned my head to look, and sure enough, it was Jessica in the driver's seat. She saw me, and when she did, she hastily put her car in drive and took off in the other direction.

After the slashed tire came the cutting of my phone line. I woke up one morning to find that my home telephone wasn't working. After checking all the wires in the house, I went outside to check on the phone wires outside. I found that the phone line had been cut. I immediately called the police to report it. The officer arrived and looked at it. He decided to go to talk to a few of my neighbors to find out if they had seen anything.

The one neighbor across the street told the officer that she had seen someone walking around outside my house after dark with a flashlight. Unfortunately, there isn't much you can do if you can't prove who did it. By this point, they were making it very clear that they were always within arm's reach of me. From following my family and I to a restaurant, to following me all day while I ran errands, going to the post office, to McDonald's, where they would jab a five-inch nail into my tire.

It looked like they had succeeded at this point in sending me the message that I wasn't safe and that they were always there right behind me. They started stalking me for hours a day. The person stalking me drove a silver Chevy Avalanche pickup truck around my house for hours and hours all day and night. They spent the entire day driving circles around my house. Every time I stepped outside to pick up my newspaper from the driveway, the same silver Chevy Avalanche would drive be driving by again. It had a very loud gasoline engine. I could hear the engine as it slowly circled my house, over and over again while I sat on the couch watching TV, or was in the kitchen cooking something to eat. It was outlandish and very aggravating.

Tiffany and her evil team of bullies spent several weeks doing this. I would sometimes be outside when they drove by and I would wave to them. I got so used to the sound of the engine circling my house for so many hours every day that I usually just ignored it, until one time I could hear the engine running, but the sound wasn't moving. The sound of the engine had become stationary, and the sound was coming from the front of the house.

I decided to go look out the window to see what they were doing. The truck was stopped in the street in front of my mailbox, doing something to it. When I saw this, I grabbed a baseball bat and opened the door and started walking down the driveway towards the mailbox and the truck. When they saw me coming towards them, they immediately stopped whatever it was that they were trying to do with my mailbox and took off, tearing down the mail box as they sped away. Again, I reported it to the police, gave them a description of the Silver Chevy Avalanche, and once again they couldn't do anything about it. This happened to occur on an afternoon when my son was with his mother. The very next day I was scheduled to pick him up.

The next morning my dad and I picked Jonathan up, and we were curious to see if he knew anything about the mailbox, to prove to ourselves that it was his mother that did it. So rather than take him home, where he would obviously see the mailbox knocked down on the ground, we took him straight to McDonald's to eat breakfast.

While we were there, my dad asked him if he knew about anything that had happened to daddy's house. My dad didn't mention the mailbox specifically, nor did he mention that anything happened, nor did he mention any time frame. He simply asked my son, Jonathan, if he knew about anything happening to daddy's house. My son's reply would once again prove that it was his mother. He replied to my dad by saying, "Daddy's mailbox was knocked down." My dad and I looked at each other, and we didn't say any more about it.

Tiffany and I had agreed, via court agreement to attend family counseling once a month. During the counseling session that occured about a week after my mailbox was knocked down, she decided to bring a gift for me. I kid you not, she brought a mailbox that she had painted. Tiffany told me she was making them for family, friends and to sell online, and she thought I would like one. It was obvious that she was trying to be a condescending and wanted to rub it in my face that she had done it. As if to say, ha ha, I did it, what are you going to do about it? Wow...

Tiffany was emboldened and had no problem letting me know that it was her doing this. We were assigned by the courts to go to an assigned family counselor named Tina. She proved to be a liar and as corrupt as they come. I also didn't know that Tiffany chose this counselor because her family knew her. I told the counselor what had been happening, with the silver Chevy Avalanche stalking me, my phone line being cut, and tire being slashed and how I thought it had something to do with Tiffany and Jessica.

During the counseling session I also decided to tell Tiffany about what was happening, playing dumb, pretending like I didn't know it was her. I told her there was someone stalking me and vandalizing my home, and that I was sharing this with her because I wanted her to know what was happening because I was concerned that our son could be in danger.

I told her that I had placed cameras all around my house, which I did, and I also bluffed and told her I had talked to my neighbor across the street and that she allowed me to put cameras on her house, facing my home. I also told her that I hired a private investigator, which I didn't, to spend some time trying to catch the silver Chevy Avalanche stalking me and to try to get its tag and run it to find out who owns the vehicle. I had done all this with the thought that if I told her about all the cameras and PI, that she would hopefully give up and leave me alone. So sure enough, immediately after sharing this with her, the silver Chevy Avalanche disappeared, for at least a week.

It had been circling my house every day for quite a while. Now, all of a sudden, it's gone, and I didn't see it for about a week. At first, I thought it worked, and that I scared her off. I was wrong. It wasn't long before the truck began its routine again. Day after day, driving around my house for hours. My friend Daniel would always tell me that they were stupid. They were wasting their money on gas, wasting their time and that sooner or later they would get tired and eventually leave me alone. He was referring to Jessica. Knowing that Jessica and I had nothing connecting us, like Tiffany and I had with our son, she would eventually just give up and leave me alone. While that did eventually prove to be true, the obsession that Tiffany had with me would not end anytime soon.

The next surprise that they had for me, was waiting on the doorstep of my lanai in the back yard. I woke up one morning and went outside in my backyard to find a dead fish lying on the doorstep of my lanai. I picked it up and tossed it in the trash, not thinking anything of it. I just assumed that it was some kid having fun and playing a prank. Later that day, I mentioned it to my dad on the phone, and he asked me if I knew what it meant.

I was like, "What are you talking about?" He said, "Do you know what a dead fish on your doorstep means?" I was honestly perplexed. I said, "No". He told me it was a death threat. He went on to tell me that the mafia would lay a dead fish, usually wrapped in newspaper, on the doorstep of someone they were threatening to kill. That's when I realized it wasn't some random kid playing a prank. I don't remember if I reported this to the police, like I had with the mailbox and phone line, but I had become aware of the fact that the police couldn't do anything anyway and I was on my own.

Chapter Twenty

Mommy Hurts Me

In May 2005, I picked up Jonathan. It was a day that I wasn't supposed to pick him up. His mother called me asking if I could pick him up, and I agreed. My mom and I picked him up and brought him to my mom's house. It wasn't long after picking him up that he blurted out, "Mommy hurts me". We looked him over and saw bruises, deep angry-looking welts all over his arms and legs. We asked him about it and he told us that he woke up in the middle of the night and knocked on his mother's bedroom door. She got mad and pinched him real, real hard, several times. Using his left hand, he demonstrated how she squeezed and pinched his arms and legs. Looking at the bruises, you could clearly see that they were caused by several fingers and a thumb.

Mom and I were concerned because this wasn't the first time he came to us injured. There was the time a little over a year earlier that he came home with a severe burn on his hand, but he was so young he couldn't talk at that time. Now he was old enough to talk, and he wasn't afraid to talk, but unfortunately, no one cared to listen. We decided to contact the police to document it.

As mentioned before, my attorney advised me to document everything of significance. Events that had taken place before, and events that would take place just a couple of years later would prove that she had no problem hurting him and then turning around and falsely accusing me of doing it. We felt that documenting it immediately after picking him up would at least prove that the injury was already there when we picked him up, so the next day when we returned him to her, she couldn't say that she picked him up from us with injuries on him and accuse me of doing it.

The sheriffs' office sent out an officer. His name was Tony Moretti. He came in, looked at my son, and the bruises, and as always, just because it was only bruises and nothing major like broken bones, they would usually disregard it, saying that it was no big deal. Understandably, there is usually no way of knowing if it was abuse, or simply a child falling and getting hurt. The reason why we reported this was because he told us how it happened. While talking to the officer outside, I explained to him what my son had told us. He came in, made a couple of calls and took out his laptop to start writing up his report. At this point he made it clear that it was no big deal and not to worry about it.

While he was sitting at the table writing his report, my son is walking around and blurts out again, "My mommy hurts me". The officer hears him say this and I look at him and say, "Don't waste your breath Jonathan, nobody cares". The officer replied to me, "You don't have to be sarcastic", then I said, "Well it's true isn't it?'

He said nothing and continued writing his report. While he was writing his report, I told him that my son's mother and I had been going to a family counselor, per our most recent court order, in an attempt to try to establish and maintain healthy communication between the two of us in order to better parent our son. When I told him the name of the counselor, Tina Brown, he stopped typing and turn his head and looked right at me then asked me to go outside with him.

I followed him outside and he began to tell me about his experience with Tina Brown. He told me that he recently went through a divorce and that he and his ex-wife had gone to marriage counseling with Tina Brown. She testified in court at his divorce hearing, and made up lies about him, twisting things against him and basically screwing him over on purpose.

When he opened up and confided in me, I told him that Tina was doing the same thing to me. You see, just a couple of weeks earlier, I had to report another incident of concern when my son came home and told me and my parents that his mother was hurting him. The DCFS investigator, Kirsten Daniels, had asked me to sign a release allowing Tina Brown to discuss the counseling sessions that Tiffany and I had with her. I would end up obtaining a copy of Kirsten's report, where she states that Tina Brown told her that I said a bunch of stuff that I never said.

Tina made up stories to convince Kirsten that Tiffany had done nothing to our son, to protect her, and sweep the child abuse under the rug. This woman, this corrupt, lying, messed up counselor, had aided and abetted in the abuse of my son. As I mentioned earlier in this book, I later found out that Tina was a friend of Tiffany's brother-in-law, hence the favor she was doing for Tiffany.

Anyway, the officer continued to tell me about when he was abused as a kid too. He said he had dishes broken over the top of his head, and while he understood that any abuse to a child is horrific, I should be glad it's only bruises and not as bad as what he went through. He told me to hang in there and some day it will all get better

A few days later, Kirsten Daniels responded to the report that Officer Moretti sent into her office and came knocking on my door at 7:30 in the morning to do a home visit. Long story short, she had bought all the crap that the lying, corrupt counselor Tina Brown had sold her and even though Officer Moretti saw the bruises on my son, heard my son tell him directly that his mother was hurting him and stated all of this in his report, she had already made up her mind.

Kirsten had already decided that she was going to do what she did for a living, sweep the truth under the rug, look the other way and always protect her own. After she left, my son and I were sitting on the couch watching cartoons, when he looked up at me and asked me, "Daddy, are you telling the nice lady what is happening to me?" All I could do was say "Yes" and change the channel to distract him and divert his attention to the TV. There was nothing more that I could do or say. Nothing is more frustrating than knowing your child lives in abuse and you can't do anything about it! I was helpless.

Chapter Twenty-One
Nearly Fatal Attraction

It was June 2005, when the very best attempt to destroy me was made. It was late at night, around 10:00 PM. when I was driving home from the store one night. This was the night they would make their first serious attempt at taking my life. I was driving north on Hills Blvd, which back in 2005, was just a dirt road with no stop signs and no stoplights. I turned right on to my street, San Pedro Drive, and noticed there was an SUV on each one of the empty corner lots.

As I turned onto San Pedro Drive, they both began following me towards my house. I knew they were following me, so rather than turn into my driveway, I decided to continue driving and turn left just past my house. I then circled around the block until I got back on San Pedro Drive going the opposite direction of my home, back towards Hills Blvd.

They continued to follow me. As I pulled up to the intersection of San Pedro Drive and Hills Blvd, there was yet another vehicle, a pickup truck on the empty corner lot on Hills Blvd just a hundred feet on the left.

I had only made a brief stop at the intersection, maybe for a half of a second at most and then continued as I took a right turn going north on Hills Blvd.

As I began my drive north on Hills Blvd, they started to speed up really fast, as they continued to pursue me. I had no idea where I would be going. My heart was pounding as I considered my options.

I had a two-car garage at home, but it was filled with boxes and totes of old winter clothes and work-related office supplies and furniture. Going home would've required me getting out of my car in the middle of the driveway, and I knew I wouldn't have time to get inside the house before several of them would jump out of their trucks and do who knows what to me. I didn't know if they had guns, knives or baseball bats, but I'm sure they didn't come empty handed. I began to realize that their initial plan was probably to catch me getting out of my car in my driveway. I knew that going home wasn't an option.

As I continued driving north on Hills Blvd, they began chasing me at speeds of 80 plus miles an hour, on what was a busted-up dirt road, with very little pavement, and a speed limit of 40 mph.

As I look back on this night, I can't help but to think of how this all reminds me of the Grand Theft Auto Games. In these video games the character that you control can go racing up and down the highways, and then jump out of the car and go shoot someone or beat someone to death. It was so surreal, I felt like I was living inside of the game that night.

Now with speeds of more than 80 miles per hour, it would appear as though their goal at this time was to run me off of the road, into a ditch, or a tree, where once it happened, if I survived the wreck, they could drag me out of my truck and finish off the job and leave me on the side of the road to die.

After several minutes of racing north on Hills Blvd., I realize that I'm going to be approaching the end of the road soon. When I got to the end of the road, I turned my truck right around without stopping and headed back south in the opposite direction. I suppose I could've taken a right or left, but when you have just a split second to make a choice, you randomly pick one direction and just put the pedal to the medal and drive.

As I'm driving south approaching 90 miles an hour and I now have three vehicles chasing me, I began to approach the other end of the road and again I quickly make a u-turn and head back north on Hills Blvd. I continued driving as fast as I could, and while I was doing so, I reached my hand into my pocket to grab my cell phone, and as I flip it open, the screen lights up. As I'm beginning to head back north, there are two of the three trucks right behind me and the third one was just passing me going the opposite direction, about to make its u turn as well.

I have to assume it was at this moment, when the third vehicle and I crossed paths, that the driver saw the phone light up in my hand and assumed that I was calling the police, in which case he or she would be assuming correctly.

I dialed 911 and the operator answered and asked me what my emergency was. I told her that I was driving home when three trucks began following me and were trying to run me off the road. I remember telling her that we were going over 80 miles an hour. She asked me what cross street I was approaching or had just passed so she could pinpoint where I was. After a few minutes, she found that there was a police officer doing a traffic stop on one of the cross streets ahead of me. She told me to turn right on Ashland Blvd as I approached it.

When I reached the street, I made the turn and the three trucks continued to go straight, apparently abandoning their pursuit of me. As I was driving east on Ashland Blvd, I kept looking in my rear-view mirror to see if they were behind me. I presumed that they were trying to figure out a way to take another road going east and then try to catch up with me down the road. About a mile and a half down Ashland Blvd I finally see the police officer on the side of the road. I still had the 911 operator on the phone. I told her I saw the officer's lights flashing on the side of the road.

She told me to pull up and park behind him and that he would be able to assist me. When I finally stopped the car, I got out and approached the officer. He had already been updated about the situation from the 911 operator. After such an adrenaline rush my body just went limp. I have no idea what my heart rate and blood pressure were, but I knew they were probably off the charts. The police officer was very professional. He knew the incredible stress I had just experience and speaking to him had a calming effect on me. He told me to stay there with him for a while and began to take all the information for a report to be filed.

He asked me to describe everything that had happened, just like I'm explaining right now, and asked if I could give him a description of the vehicles and the drivers. The only thing I had seen regarding any of the drivers was when it first started, and I was arriving home and turned onto my street, the one SUV on the left corner lot had its window open. There was a guy in the driver's seat with his left arm hanging out of the window. It was a very light skinned male with a medium build. I didn't get a look at the face though. The officer followed me to my house after taking the report.

My son wasn't with me that night of course, he was with his mom. I suppose Tiffany probably left him with her mom or one of her sisters while we had fun playing real life GTA.

I woke up that next morning trying to figure out what happened the night before. Was it a bad dream? No, it actually happened.

I was scheduled to pick up Jonathan from his mom the morning after the chase, so my parents went with me to pick him up. I remember the look on Tiffany's face at the pickup, she looked disappointed.   After that, we all went to my sister's house. She only lived about five miles away from me.

When Jonathan and I went back to my sister's house, he had something very interesting to say.   He was only two-and-a-half years old at this time, but had begun speaking in full sentences at sixteen months old.

He began saying, "Daddy won't miss you, daddy won't miss you." He was chanting it all day, just randomly blurting out "Daddy won't miss you".

It was obvious Tiffany had told him the day before that "daddy won't miss you", just before she tried to kill me.

I was always kind of confused about that, wondering why she would tell him the day before that daddy won't miss you, because her intent was to murder me. Had she succeeded, I'd be dead, and a dead man isn't going to miss anyone. I never really understood it until many years later.

In 2013, I met my wife Erica.   Erica was someone I could pour out my heart to. She was a patient, wonderful listener. We married after dating awhile. Ultimately, it was Erica's interpretation of what my son said that would make the most sense.

When I told Erica the story of the time my son's mother tried to kill me, I told her what Jonathan said the next day, and how I didn't understand how to interpret it.   Erica's opinion was that Tiffany probably told my son, "Daddy won't miss you" repeatedly the day of the attempted murder. Tiffany was presuming that she would succeed later that night, and probably told my son that his daddy had left him and wasn't coming back.

Tiffany must have had a whole plan in place to say that I took off somewhere and just abandoned Jonathan.

In her evil delight, she just kept saying, "Daddy's not going to miss you. He went away somewhere and he's not coming back".

Tiffany's plan was to play the victim. When people would ask her? "Where is Jonathan's dad?"

Tiffany would answer, "I don't know. He just stopped calling or inquiring about Jonathan. He left so he wouldn't have to pay child support. He's a deadbeat father."

She certainly wasn't going to tell her son that his dad was dead, or that she did it. Tiffany was very confident that she would get the job done. Tiffany didn't know about the promise that God had made to me, to bring my son home someday. Had she known, and had she been a wise person, she wouldn't have bothered trying to destroy something that God had built. Her efforts were worthless. No different than the devil's efforts to defeat God.

At least the devil knows he can't win, but that doesn't stop him from trying to cause as much damage as possible while he still can. Tiffany thought she could win. It is the evil of the devil that drives people to do the evil things they do. She believed that she could succeed.

Even the devil didn't know God's plan for my life. Had he known, would he have spent the time trying so hard to destroy me through her? What good would a murder attempt do if it was impossible to begin with? Seems like it's just proof that the devil doesn't know everything. His knowledge is limited. His power is restricted. His authority is reduced to only to what God allows it to be.

Chapter Twenty-Two
Midnight Stalkers

The summer of 2005 was very memorable, but for all the wrong reasons. My friend Daniel had come up in late June to spend the summer at my house again. He was still attending college in northern Florida. He came down a little too late to enjoy the attempt on my life, but he was here just in time for a lot of other exciting activities. Daniel and I would have fun on 'stakeouts', sitting in my truck out in my driveway, late at night, waiting for them to come around.

We went out there two or three times a week. I would have the truck backed into the driveway, facing the street, with a sunshade on the dashboard. We would end up catching them around my house several times. There was one night that they were in a white car when they drove up to my house in the middle of the night, stopping right in front of my home. They let a young guy out of the car right at the end of my driveway. When the guy got out of the car, Daniel and I took down the sunshade, and at that point I'm sure he saw that we were in the truck because he started running.

He ran into an empty wooded lot across the street. I started the truck and we drove around to see if we could find him. Neither one of us were interested in pursuing him on foot. We drove around for about twenty minutes and couldn't find him. We retreated back to the driveway and sat in the truck for about another hour or two, waiting to see if he came back. I'm sure he had run a block or two away and called for his accomplices to come pick him up. I'm not sure what the intent was that night.

Maybe to slash my tires again, or throw a brick through the window of my home, who knows?

Daniel was able to get the license plate of the vehicle that night. I had an account with a web-based program that allowed users to do background checks, and one of the features available was the ability to run license plates.

We were able to locate the owner of the vehicle. The next day we drove by the owner's house, which happened to be just a few miles away from my home, in order to check it out. It was a nice house with an underground pool in the back yard. The family was apparently having a cookout the next afternoon when we drove by. There were a lot of people there. We saw someone that looked like the young guy from the night before. We ran a background check on the owner of the vehicle and found nothing. Clean as a whistle. It was fun and exciting to catch them in the act, and it was good to have been able to prevent them from accomplishing whatever it was that they had planned on that night.

Another one of the most memorable nights that summer, was when Daniel and I were once again out in the truck in the driveway late at night. A dark green pickup truck came driving by the house. We noticed that it started to circle around the block, driving by the house again and again. Then it started to drive by slowly. We had the sunshade on the window, and I'm guessing that they were trying to see if anyone was in my truck. Daniel and I decided to start up the truck and start driving. When we pulled out of the driveway we turned right, towards Hills Blvd.

The green truck must have been on the side street to our left at that moment, because a few moments later it turned onto San Pedro Drive and ended up right behind us. We decided to drive at a normal rate of speed as we headed down the road. We took some turns to see if the truck would follow us, and sure enough, it did. After the first few turns, when it kept following us, the speed began to pick up a little bit. After a few miles of driving, there was finally a moment when we were able to turn things around and go from being the hunted, to the hunter.

I don't remember exactly what street we were on at the time, but we were able to get behind them and started to follow them. We ended up on Venetian Blvd, as we followed behind them. We were approaching an intersection when they decided to drive into the left turning lane and just as they began to drive into the left turning lane, the light turned red. So rather than follow them and stop behind them at the light, I went into the straight lane, and stopped at the light beside them. Now while their windows were very darkly tinted, I was able to see that there was a woman in the passenger's seat. I couldn't see any facial details through the dark windows.

All I could see was her long hair, and the fact that she turned her head to look at us. She was turning her head back and forth, with her hair flipping all around. I'm sure she was probably afraid that I could see that it was her. When the light turned green, they turned left, and I drove straight. By that time, I decided not to pursue them any longer, and I figured that they were probably not going to pursue me any longer either. I think that this encounter at least let them know that I wasn't afraid of them. I later would run the tag of the pickup truck and found that the truck was owned by a young guy with a criminal record a mile long. There were arrests for drugs, burglary, even attempted rape.

The rest of the summer would continue like this. The silver Chevy Avalanche would continue circling my house almost every day. While it was certainly a crazy summer, I must admit that it was never really concerning to me. I was cautious, but not afraid. I was prepared, but not shaken. My God had proven Himself mighty in my defense. He can always be counted on. How grateful I am for His faithfulness!

The summer wouldn't end without at least one more memorable event taking place. It was sometime in late August, after Daniel had already gone back to college. It was late at night, probably after midnight. I was on the couch watching TV when the doorbell rang. I had security cameras setup around the outside of the house with a DVR and monitors in the kitchen. I immediately went to the monitors to see who was outside my front door in the middle of the night. It was dark, but I was able to see that it was a young male, and he was wearing a baseball cap, and had dark sunglasses on. I immediately ran to my room to get my gun and returned to the kitchen where I sat and watched this guy on the monitor. He rang the doorbell several more times. And after several minutes had passed by, he finally walked back to his car.

He had parked his car in my driveway and turned the lights off before he drove into the driveway. When he got back in the car and started it, he proceeded to drive in reverse to pull out of my driveway while he kept the headlights off, so that he or his car wouldn't be visible. With the lights on outside my garage, and the brake lights on the car, I was able to see that it was an older, full size vehicle, most likely a Buick. I didn't call the police. I figured that it would take about twenty minutes for the police to arrive, and by that point, the guy in the baseball cap would've either accomplished what he and his friends had come here for, or he would've left. Either way, the police wouldn't have been able to help.

The circumstances of this event make me wonder what their intention was on this night. I know I've wondered about it. Driving up in my driveway after midnight, with a hat and sunglasses on in the middle of the night, knocking on my door. I suppose they expected me to walk up to the door, open it up, and invite them in for a cup of coffee. Really! I don't think so. Opening the door would not have accomplished anything good. They would've had a baseball bat or a gun. There were probably a few more of them in the car waiting to jump out. Did they really think I was that stupid? I imagine that at best, it would've ended up with one or more of them dead, and me trying to explain to the police that I was defending myself. Or at worst, me dead and then that would have been the end of the story. Well anyway, they left that night, and all was well.

Chapter Twenty-Three
Swimming with the Sharks

Things had gotten out of control that summer, and it appeared as though they weren't going to stop their relentless pursuit of my life. I was running out of ideas on how to protect myself. I bought a gun earlier in the summer of 2005. It was the best thing I could've done at that point. I honestly never had any desire to own a gun. I never thought I would buy one. It was out of complete necessity that I purchased one. When someone tries to kill you, it makes you look at the second amendment in a whole different way. It made me appreciate it a whole lot more.

My frustration with the legal system had grown. The police couldn't do anything to protect me or my son. A horrifically corrupt judicial system had failed us so many times. I decided that I would work to try to make a change in our state's outdated and discriminatory laws. I had no interest in become a police officer, as I already had a full-time career that I wasn't ready to give up on just yet. I had never been to college, and I wasn't a lawyer, so being a judge wasn't possible. The only thing that I saw as being a possibility was politics.

I knew I needed to start small, like city commissioner, or the county school board, but I was in a hurry. I needed to be able to make changes that simply couldn't wait the years and years that it would take to make it to the top in the traditional way. The traditional way would've taken years of "paying your dues" as it was described to me, and years of kissing the behinds of the political party leaders in our community and the people that control the campaign dollars. I simply didn't have the time it took to start at the bottom and work my way to the top.

I decided that I would set my sights a little higher and make a run for our state legislature. I was only twenty-nine years old at the time. I realized that my age all by itself would be a challenge, considering I lived in a county where the median age was over sixty years old. I was in Florida, or as others described it, 'God's waiting room'. Never having been to college would also be a strike against me. I had never played the game, never kissed up to the party's leaders, never been a team player, and had honestly never even been a part of the team. I literally came out of nowhere, wanting to take a seat on the legislature away from a much older, much wealthier business owner that had won it just a year earlier. He had a tough race in 2004 against a doctor and had just barely won by less than one percent to secure the victory. I wasn't really planning on announcing my intent to run anytime in 2005. I was planning on waiting until the spring of 2006.

However, the stalking, attempted murder, etc. was getting so intense, that I was beginning to be legitimately concerned for my life. It was my reasoning that if I shined a spotlight on myself, more and more people would notice me. The theory was that it would make it harder for Tiffany and Jessica to continue their menacing ways, because more people would be watching me.

It became a lot likelier that they too would get noticed, which they certainly didn't want for themselves and all of their criminal mischief. Out of a sense of desperation, I decided to file the paperwork in August 2005. I'm not sure if doing so helped at all, but they did begin to cease and desist at around the same time that I announced my intent to run. It's possible that my plan had worked.

I remember receiving a call from the incumbent, George Sanders, just a couple of days later. He invited me to lunch at one of his favorite Thai restaurants in town. He asked me why I was running. I told him that I had no intention of winning, and that my goal was to have a voice, a voice that otherwise would never have been heard. When you call your legislators office with a concern, do you really think he or she would take the time to meet with you? No, of course they wouldn't. At least most of them wouldn't.

I was told by an older, retired legislator from Missouri, when you call your legislator's office, they will have their assistant take your name and number. Then he or she would look your name up on their donor list. And guess what, if they didn't see your name on their donor list for the last election, you probably wouldn't receive a call back.

You might receive some generic email thanking you for contacting their office, assuring you that your legislator will be working hard to fight for your needs, blah, blah, blah, blah. I was already aware of the fact that I wouldn't get anyone's attention until I stood face to face with them and threatened to take away what was theirs. I did that when I filed the papers to establish my intent to run. As anticipated, it worked. It got me a seat at the table with my legislator. I expressed the reasons for my run, and humbly explained that I did not have any intention of winning. I did ask him that when it was all done, if he would at least be willing to represent my interests and address my concerns with some legislative changes, by filing a bill to update the outdated and discriminatory laws.

Campaigning was a blast. Things didn't really pick up until the late spring of 2006. There were tons of speaking engagements, debates, candidate forums and interviews with the newspapers and local television network affiliates. There was so much going on that I'm sure I will never be able to remember everything. I would love to share with you some of the highlights.

I'll never forget my first ever candidate's forum. It was at a college in my district. It happened to be a room filled with Democrats. No offense to Democrats, but I happen to be a Republican, and so without a single Republican in the audience, the response I received to some of the answers I had given were quite frightening.

I thought I was going to get lynched on my way out that evening. I tend to be brutally honest, and lack the ability to bend the truth, or to sugar coat it. You ask me a question, and you will receive an honest answer. I may not have been so good at being politically correct. I don't remember all the questions specifically, but I'm sure there were some questions pertaining to taxes and management of our state's finances.

As a tax advisor, and business owner, I tend to be very financially responsible and would reflect that characteristic in my answers to any such questions. I do remember one question that was asked about abortion, and if I would support pro-life legislation. My response was a little too blunt, when I said, "As a legislator, I will not have the blood of our children on my hands". You should have seen the stone-cold stares received from everyone in that audience. It's hard to be an honest person in politics. And because of this, it would appear as though I was doomed for failure.

One of the funniest memories I have from the campaign occurred at a debate that took place at the North Harbor Yacht club. My opponent had opened the event with the introduction of another gentleman that was running for the state senate. That gentleman was a bit younger than my opponent, probably in his late thirties or early forties. When he introduced the man and brought him up to the podium, he had made a comment during the introduction, saying that "We need some fresh young blood in Tallahassee." I thought it was ironic that he would say that, considering that I was twenty-nine years old and he was about twice my age.

When it was my turn to get up and speak, I opened with a comment on how my opponent and I don't agree about much, other than one thing. And I said, "My opponent was 100 percent accurate when he said that we needed some fresh young blood in Tallahassee, and I thank him so much for his endorsement of me." It was funny, it cut the tension in the air, and we all had a good laugh

During the summer of campaigning, I met a handful of wonderful people. The first one was Bryan Cooper. He was a doctor and a legislator in the neighboring district. I ended up becoming acquainted with him though the campaign and we kept in touch for a few years after. He was a great person, and a wonderful mentor. He shared his wisdom and experience with me, which meant a lot to me, considering I didn't have a clue as to what I was doing. He was also a great friend to me when my dad had to retire from his job and lost his health insurance for six months until he qualified for Medicare. He provided medical treatment for my dad several times for free.

Then there was Gary. I met him when I was having dinner at a restaurant. He had seen my campaign shirt and came over to introduce himself to me. He asked me about my campaign, so I invited him to join me at my table and we talked. He had expressed similar political opinions and expressed an interest in working with me. We ended up working together on the campaign and he assisted me with various campaign functions, such as distributing signs and literature.

I also met a very interesting man named Charles Turner during the campaign. He was a Vietnam veteran, and a legislator in his home state of Missouri many years earlier. Having been in the position that I was running for, he had a lot of great advice and opinions. He would end up assisting me throughout the campaign and we would be acquainted for several years, until his death in 2008.

We typically met for lunch and talked about the campaign. One time he brought me a brochure that my opponent had mailed out to the community. He seemed to have enjoyed the fact that I was making this guy work hard to hold on to his job. I had assumed that he wasn't taking this seriously. After all, he had raised about $150,000 for his campaign from the people that controlled the Republican party in our district. He was the party's chosen one.

I had raised almost no money and ended up spending about $15,000 of my own money just to have some fun. I never thought I would win, but I was having fun along the way. Like I said, I met a lot of great people along the way, from state senators to U.S. Congressmen. Not that it did me much good in the end. The changes I wanted to see made to the Florida laws were not "politically correct". The thought of offering equal rights to both mothers and fathers was unacceptable. The thought of guaranteeing children of divorced and separated parents the right to have equal time with both their mom and dad was absurd.

At the time of our separation, Florida courts would only give primary custody to mothers. Trying to change society's perspective of this was like trying to convince them that Santa Claus was real. None of the legislators I had become acquainted with would touch this with a ten-foot pole. At least not if they wanted to get re-elected.

It's a shame that nothing meaningful ever gets done in our state or federal governments because of the corrupt ways of our political system. It's too much to get into right here and now, but maybe, just maybe you might read about my political ideas and opinions in another book.

My opponent ended up taking this campaign much more seriously than I thought. As I was hitting the streets, knocking on a few doors, I learned from a gentleman that I spoke with that my opponent had already been to his house to visit. It appeared he was hitting the streets as well.

As it got closer to the election day, interest in the campaign had grown. I became more and more noticed, obviously not by the amount of money I spent on advertising, because I only had ten percent of the budget that my opponent had, but because of the message I was delivering. I did very little paid advertising, almost none.

I was getting free coverage from the media. That was all the exposure I had. The Tribune was a newspaper company owned by liberals. They didn't like me because I was extremely conservative. Their references to me were always a little less than flattering.

The Herald on the other hand was the larger of the two newspapers in the area at the time, and they loved me. They obviously couldn't endorse me even though they wanted to. They had to follow the party's chosen one. However, when I met the owner of the newspaper, the meeting went very well. He loved the message I was delivering, and we talked for a while and he ended up offering me an opportunity to write for the newspaper.

I would take him up on the offer right after the campaign ended, by writing a column for the paper once a week. He was willing to allow me to write a daily column, something that I probably should have taken advantage of. This was certainly a missed opportunity on my part, because after only two or three months I stopped writing. They loved everything I had written and submitted, publishing it all. Initially I was only being published in the local edition of the newspaper. But there was one article they liked so much that they published it in the local edition of the newspaper as well as in several other neighboring counties.

On election night of 2006, I spent the day visiting the polling locations, talking to people and shaking hands. It had been a long, exhausting day. I had fallen ill just a few weeks earlier, and I mean severely ill. I had almost lost my life and was struggling with some severe health challenges. But I forced myself to go out all day and work, when I should have been in the hospital. My son was with me that day, and my parents were taking care of him. They dropped him off at my home when I was finished working. It was around 8 o'clock at night, and I had just put Jonathan to bed.

I had gotten a call from Gary several hours earlier because he was watching the news and saw that it was reported that I had received 44 percent of the votes thus far with only a portion of the total votes having been counted. It appeared as though, at this point at least, that this might potentially be more than just fun and games. I had a chance to actually win.

Considering the fact that I was challenging the incumbent, and I was being outspent ten to one, coming anywhere close to 50 percent of the votes would have been very flattering. While I was trying to keep my expectations real, my friend Charles had a much different opinion. You see, he was very well connected to the Republican party in our district. He heard all the chatter that was being said about me and the campaign. That evening, before the results were announced, he called me, and we spent at least an hour on the phone.

He was telling me that I was going to win. He gave me all the details, everything that he heard, and told me about all the chatter that was going on about me. I was entertained at the thought of winning and trusted his opinion because of his experience and his connection to the local party.

What was interesting is that later that night, when all the votes were counted, I was announced as the winner of the Florida House of Representatives race. It was announced on all the news networks, all the local network affiliates, Fox, ABC, CBS, and NBC news. However, it wasn't long after I was announced as the winner that my phone rang, and it was the Herald newspaper. The reporter asked me for my comments on having lost the race. I was confused to say the least. Just twenty or thirty minutes earlier I was announced as the winner by every television network in the southwest Florida area.

I asked the reporter what he had as the results from the local supervisor of elections office. He said that I had lost in a 73-27 percent vote count. I presumed that he was accurate and proceeded with giving him my comments. Mr. Turner wasn't convinced that I lost this race. For days and days after election day he kept telling me to go to the supervisor of elections office to find out what the "real" numbers were. People were congratulating me for the victory, even months after the election was over. Everyone had seen on television that I was announced as the winner, and I had to tell everyone that what they had seen on tv was wrong, and I actually didn't win after all. It was quite a disappointing situation.

Unfortunately for me, in 2006, Florida only had electronic voting machines with no paper ballets, with no paper trail at all. No way to verify the vote count. If the supervisor of elections said you lost, then you lost. It was as simple as that. You had to trust an elected official, and trust that the computers that counted the votes were accurate. I'm sure that it was all just a big misunderstanding. It was just like Steve Harvey announcing the wrong winner at the Miss Universe contest in 2015. It happens.

A similar situation occurred in our district's U.S. House race in this election cycle. The U.S. House race had 16,000 under votes in one specific city in this district. What this means is that out of approximately 30,000 people from this city that voted in the 2006 election, more than half of them allegedly chose to cast their ballots, and vote for every other race on the ballet except for the US house race, leaving one candidate to narrowly win the race by just a fraction of a percent. Again, no paper ballots and no paper trail. I remember the losing party tried to challenge the results, but to no avail.

I'm not trying to be a conspiracy theorist, I'm simply stating the facts. You do with the facts what you wish. A couple of weeks after the election, I was hanging out with Bryan Cooper at his office, and he told me that he had been flooded with calls for about two weeks prior to the election, with people asking him about me, and that it was believed that I was going to win. From what he told me, the leaders of the Republican party and the big money people weren't so excited about that. I suppose they had done polls, and the polls might have caused them some concern. I didn't have enough money to conduct any polls myself.

Another thing to note is that in Florida, we have what is called early voting. You have two weeks before an election to cast your vote, whereas in most states, you have only one day to cast your vote, on election day. With approximately 50% of votes being cast by the night before election day, the supervisor of elections office had a pretty good idea of who was going to win the race in their county. By the time we got to the end of our conversation, Bryan told me that in his opinion, something wasn't right with the results of my election.

Chapter Twenty-Four
Day Care Nightmares

The next twelve months after the election were relatively calm. There were of course the usual unexplainable injuries on my son, the incessant threats and false accusations here and there. My son and I were constantly dealing with screaming and chaos at the pickups and drop offs. It was a crazy, stressful way for Jonathan and I to live.

On a brighter note, the intense stalking, vandalism and attempts on my life had come to an end. I'm guessing that Jessica had gotten bored with trying to kill me, and probably set her sights on someone else, leaving Tiffany to be obsessed with me all by herself. Nothing too far out of the ordinary had happened during this time. At least not until around September 2007.

It was approximately September 2007, and Tiffany had a full-time job working as a worker's comp insurance claims adjuster. She worked a regular 9:00 AM-5:00 PM shift Monday through Friday, and on the days she had Jonathan, she would leave him at daycare. Years before that in 2004, I'd had some concerns about the daycare that I had brought to Tiffany's attention and to the court's attention. I hadn't been to the daycare in years, since I had done an inspection of it back in 2004.

There was one day in September 2007 where I was driving down the road with my son, and out of nowhere he pointed down the street and said, "Daddy, that's where my daycare is". And I said, "I know Jonathan". Then he said "Daddy, do you want to go see my daycare?" I said "Sure, I'd love to", I thought it was so cute that he wanted to show me, so I agreed. He seemed so excited about it.

I was shocked by what I saw. My son and I walked in there and were greeted by one of the ladies that worked there. They didn't seem happy about being visited, and I would soon find out why. First, the place was filthy, and there was a kid wandering around with mucous dripping down from her nose, and no one had made any effort to notice her and clean her up with a tissue. It was a small house that was zoned commercial. Now as soon as I walked in with my son, I was repulsed by an intense chemical smell. When you walked in, immediately to your right there was a room with three hair salon chairs, mirrors, sinks and counters. There was a lady sitting there getting her hair dyed. Now I know I'm not a rocket scientist, but you don't have to be one to know that having babies and small toddlers in the presence of those dangerous and poisonous chemicals was probably not allowed by law.

It was horrific. I had to leave after just a minute. I literally couldn't breathe. I do have mild asthma and am usually very sensitive to chemical smells, like some perfumes, paints, and nail polish, but this was a hundred times stronger than any of the typical household chemicals that you or a family member would use daily.

After leaving, I thought it would be wise to go online and see if it was legal to have a daycare operating in the middle of a hair salon. I didn't find any information online that was conclusive enough to determine if running a daycare inside of a hair salon was legal, but I knew that the Florida Department of Children and Family Services regulated daycares.

I called DCFS to inquire about the daycare my son was in. The gentleman I spoke to at DCFS told me that Kid Kingdom daycare was not in business, and that they were not licensed. I told him that's not true, that my son was registered and attending Kid Kingdom daycare. I remember him saying "That's not possible, we shut them down a year ago". At this point, I'm becoming very concerned. He continues to tell me about the fifty-five code violations and the one hundred thousand dollars in administrative fines that had resulted in their license being revoked.

I told him that my son's mother has him enrolled in that daycare, and he has been going there for years. He then told me that the operator of the daycare cannot provide care for any children in exchange for a fee, and that without a license she can only watch up to four children, and that it can't be done inside of a hair salon. I told him my son's mother is paying for the daycare with the child support that I provide her, and he recommended that I obtain evidence of payments being made and provide it to him, to prove that the daycare was being operated illegally.

He also told me that he was the DCFS investigator that had shut down Kid Kingdom Daycare, and he told me to get my son out of there as soon as possible, that it was an awful place for any child to be. He said he wouldn't leave his dog there, let alone a human being. He wouldn't give me details, he said he wasn't allowed to by law. All he could tell me is what was already public information, such as the code violations and the fines, and the fact that it isn't licensed. He reiterated to me several more times to be sure that I get my son out of there.

After contacting DCFS to inquire about this daycare, the DCFS investigator that I spoke to went to visit the daycare, and of course, the owner lied and alleged that she was only watching four children and that she wasn't charging any of the parents for the service. So that left DCFS and me in a position where nothing could be done. I had to think of a way to get my son out of there. I thought if I emailed my son's mother, asking her if I could assist her in paying for the cost of daycare directly, in addition to the child support I was already giving her, that she would jump on the chance to get more money.

I emailed her asking her how much she was paying the daycare and asked her if she wanted me to assist. She responded in an email telling me that she pays $115 a week and to my surprise, she said she didn't need any help paying for it. Once I received her response, I immediately contacted DCFS, and forwarded them the email proving that the daycare was accepting payment for watching my son. Now after having years of experience with the authorities not being able or willing to assist and protect my son, I knew that I couldn't sit around and wait for DCFS.

I had learned from my experience in the campaign just a year or two earlier how powerful the media is. I thought if I could shine a spotlight on the daycare and on DCFS, it might light a fire underneath their feet and cause them to do their job. I contacted the local newspaper that I had worked with during the campaign and provided them the story of a daycare that had been shut down by the state of Florida and was still operating illegally.

I suggested to them that there are other parents that have their children in this daycare that might not know it was operating illegally, and that it would be in their best interest to be informed of this fact so they can protect their children. Then I sent them a copy of the email from Tiffany and sent them the contact information for the gentleman that I spoke to at DCFS.

They contacted DCFS and the daycare owner to investigate, and of course the daycare owner continued to lie, even though the newspaper had evidence to the contrary, and they published the story. I believe it was because of the spotlight that was on them that forced DCFS to act. When I first found out that the daycare was shut down, I gave Tiffany all the shocking information, with the evidence of this fact, and requested that she relocate our son to a licensed daycare facility. She refused. She insisted that keeping him at an illegal daycare that had been shut down by the state of Florida due to fifty-five code violations and $100,000 in fines was in our son's best interest.

Due to her refusal to relocate our son to a licensed and safe daycare facility, I had no choice but to spend more money on an attorney to begin the legal process of relocating our son to another daycare facility. This was pathetic. The fact that I had to spend $1,500 to force my son's mother to relocate our son to a safe and licensed daycare was insane. The fact that she refused to take him out of this illegal daycare after having knowledge of the fact that the daycare was shut down, was in my opinion child neglect and endangerment. And it wasn't unintentional neglect and endangerment, it was WILLFUL.

What kind of parent would do this to their child? I suppose the same kind of parent that would burn their kids' hand on a stove, and the same kind of parent that would abuse their child for years, and the same kind of parent that would try to murder someone for no reason, not that having a reason makes it any better. The involvement of my lawyer in this situation would end up catapulting this situation into a whole new level of danger for my son and I.

You see, after she refused to move our son to another daycare, I had to have my attorney send her a letter requesting that she change our son's daycare in order to avoid the unnecessary need for legal action. While to you and me this request seems logical and reasonable, again, the safety and best interest of our son was of no concern to her. Her only interest was power, control, and inflicting pain and destruction every chance she could.

This is what a person with Borderline Personality Disorder can do when they feel as though they have been abandoned or rejected by their significant other. I'll tell you right now, that while I'm sympathetic to the difficulties that someone with mental illness endures, I am also sympathetic with the difficulties that the family and friends of a mentally ill person endures as well. I would warn any person I meet to be careful when dating someone with this disorder. And while I know that it is not always possible to recognize the signs and symptoms of this or other mental disorders, it would be beneficial to educate yourself on the various types of mental illnesses that exist so that you can identify the possibility of the disorder in someone that you care about and try to get them treatment.

She received the letter from my attorney on a day that my son was with me, I believe it was a Saturday. The very next day, my parents, Jonathan and I were at our church for the morning service. We were scheduled to drop off my son to Tiffany right after church at the court ordered exchange location of Eckerd's Pharmacy. However, because she had become enraged at receiving the letter from my attorney, she ended up stalking us and followed us to our church.

Tiffany and her husband were waiting for us outside of the church in the parking lot. When we walked out of church, we were surprised to see them both there. They approached us, and she immediately started screaming at the top of her lungs. She was angry about the letter and was yelling and swearing in the church parking lot in front of our son. Tiffany came face to face with my mother and threatened her, and basically assaulted her.

Assault is not the act of actually hitting a person, that would be battery, assault I believe is the act of engaging in a confrontation where threats are made, and could reasonably be expected to be carried out. Our son witnessed all of this. He was so shaken by this that he was in tears. He was scared. As I'm writing this right now, I'm beginning to feel the pain that he must have gone through at that moment.

I couldn't begin to imagine what it was like for him to go through all these horrific difficulties throughout the years, nor would I ever want to know what it was like. He has been through hell. The term hell would be an understatement. No child should ever have to go through what he has been through. No matter how mentally ill a person is, I can't understand why they would they do this to their own child. It makes no sense. At least not to a mentally stable person. Maybe to the mentally ill it makes all the sense in the world to take out their own pain and frustration out on an innocent, helpless and defenseless child.

Only a coward would attack a harmless child. A coward wouldn't attack someone that can defend themselves. They care enough about themselves to not want to get hurt, but they don't care enough about others, not even their own child.

When my son was young, I would lead my son in bedtime prayers, and for years we would pray for her. Not only would we pray for her healing, but we would always pray that God would forgive her. Even while we were in the eye of the storm, we would pray for her salvation. I knew that not only is it God's will for all to be forgiven, but that her healing and salvation, had she received it, would not only benefit her, but it would benefit us too.

"The Lord is not slack concerning His promise, as some men count slackness; but is long suffering to us, not willing that any should perish, but that all should come to repentance." 2 Peter 3:9

My prayers were that her healing would cause her to stop inflicting pain and suffering upon all of us, especially Jonathan. Even at this time I still pray for her, because I know that it is our Father's will that not even one would perish. I do believe that someday she will give her life to the Lord. The reason for my faith, the reason for my hope, is the promises that He has made, and the promises that He has fulfilled. I know that He is capable of all things and that as His word has promised, that every knee shall fall, and every head will bow down before Christ.

"For it is written, as I live, saith the Lord, every knee shall bow to me, and every tongue confess to God." Romans 14:11

"That if thou shalt confess with thy mouth the Lord Jesus and shall believe in thine heart that God raised Him from the dead, thou shalt be saved. For with the mouth man believes unto righteousness; and with the mouth confession is made unto salvation." Romans 10:9-10

During her tirade in the church parking lot, she demanded to take our son with her. He was already in tears, and scared to death, so I couldn't let him walk away into the arms of his greatest fear. I didn't have to comply with her demand, because my family's church wasn't the designated exchange location. Because I wanted him to have time to calm down, I told her that I will only drop him off to her at the designated location. We all went into our cars and proceeded to drive a couple of miles down the road to the exchange location. He was still shaken up and crying during most of the car ride. I don't remember which one of us was driving, but one of us sat down in the back seat with him to try to calm him down and ease his pain.

After the drop off, we dropped my mom off at home and my dad and I drove to Tampa for a business franchise expo that we had planned on going to days earlier. It didn't take long before my phone rang with the police on the other end. The police were calling me because apparently, after stalking us and assaulting my mother, Tiffany decided to call the police and allege that my mother assaulted her. My dad and I spoke to the police officer on the phone to explain to him what happened, and the officer told me that Tiffany's husband, who happens to work for the sheriff's office, had given the officer the same version of the story that Tiffany did, therefore lying. It's nice to know that some of the people that are hired to serve and protect us are liars, cheaters, and thieves, and no better than the people they lock up. Now I know that all police officers are not like this. It's just like anything else in this world where a few bad apples spoil the bunch.

Chapter Twenty-Five

False Allegations

This incident at the church was only the first in a series of several attacks against me that were prompted by my attorney's letter to her. Now that I think about it and look at the words that I have just written, specifically the word "attacks", I realize that Tiffany could very well be described as a terrorist. The term terrorist wasn't used as often in 2007 as it is today, however she fit's the definition of the word. Dictionary.com defines "terrorist" as "A person who terrorizes or frightens others". This certainly does describe her perfectly. Currently, it's probably not appropriate to use this term loosely, however it does fit her well.

The next attack was going to be a big one. It began about a week after she received the letter from my attorney regarding the daycare. I believe it began with another phone call from the police. The police officer told me he had responded to a call from Tiffany regarding a bruise on my son's face that allegedly occurred as a result of me punching my four-year-old son in the face with a closed fist, at least that's what the police report had stated, which is a public record by the way. The night before I received the call, Tiffany had called the police at approximately 9:00 p.m. to report that our son had a bruise on his face that I had allegedly put there. I must admit that the officer that responded to her house that night had done a great job. He documented his interaction with Tiffany and my son in detail on his report.

He carefully wrote that he asked my four-year-old son what happened and how he got the bruise on his face. My son told the officer that his grandmother did it. That's exactly what the officer wrote in his report. Tiffany, I'm sure, wasn't happy about that, so she had the officer asked him again, and the second time the officer asked him he stated that his daddy did it, and illustrated how by rolling up his hand into a fist and placing it against his face.

He took photographs of the bruise and went on to send his report over to the Department of Children and Family Services, as was required by law. This false accusation became a big threat to my freedom and my future, and the future of my son. Even though she got some help from a corrupt detective in the police department, she ultimately didn't plan it out very well. You see, the day she called the police to report this, was the same day that our son had his annual physical. She had known about the physical, but apparently had forgotten about it. She never showed up at the doctor's office that afternoon. So earlier that Wednesday afternoon, my dad and I took my son to his pediatrician's office for his physical. I believe we were at Burger King before that. He loved to play at the playgrounds at Burger King and McDonalds.

He would have a blast climbing through the maze and sliding down the slide. It reminds me of some of our road trips across the country when he was younger. When it was time to stop for lunch or dinner, he would always ask me to find a McDonalds or Burger King with a playground to stop at, and I usually accommodated him. I loved to see my son having a good time, being carefree like other children. Whatever I could do to give my son happy memories with me, I did.

The visits to his pediatrician would usually be an all-day affair. They were always so busy, and we rarely ever got out of there in under three hours. I think it was around four o'clock when we got out of the office. One of the nice things about my son's pediatrician is that not only did she know that my son's mother was mentally ill, as she had witnessed some of the chaos that she created throughout the years, but she also took good notes.

Each visit would include notes about who attended, whether it was the child's mom, dad, grandfather, or grandmother. The file for the physical that day had noted that my dad was there with me and my son. After we finished at the pediatrician's office, we had some time to kill before dropping him off to his mom at 6:00pm.

My dad and I took him to the mall to play in the playground for the last hour and a half. When you're a parent, people always tell you that young children need to learn how to socialize, so I always tried to bring him to play with other kids. He was having a lot of fun and wanted to stay as long as he could. I called his mom to ask her if she would want to pick him up at the mall at 6:00pm. She agreed and came over to get him from the mall playground at 6:00pm. She would then go home and call the police several hours later.

If we wanted to play detective for a moment, in order to try to come to some sort of conclusion as to what really happened and exactly who hurt my son, we can first begin to look at the two individuals that my son named in the report that Tiffany filed that Wednesday night. I'm not a child psychologist, but I would have to draw the conclusion that the first person he named would probably have been the honest answer, and that the second person he named would have been the answer that he was coerced into saying. The first individual that he named was his grandmother.

Having had two grandmothers at the time, or maybe even three if you count his stepdad's mom, we can at least rule out my mom as an option because my mom hadn't seen my son at all that day, and my dad and I could both testify to that fact, if necessary. That would leave only his maternal grandmother and possibly his stepdad's mom. Obviously, having not been present at the time that he was hurt, I don't know for absolute certainty which one it could have been. I didn't know my son's stepdad's mother at all, I couldn't comment on her character. However, I knew my son's maternal grandmother I could tell you that her mental illness was more severe than Tiffany's.

His maternal grandmother would be the presumed individual responsible. Back in 2004 while in the hallway of the courthouse during a court mediation session, his maternal grandmother had threatened to hurt him, and sure enough, the next day that I picked him up he was injured.

Then there would be the second individual that my son named to the police office in the report that Tiffany had filed. And that would be me. Not only do I know for a fact that I didn't do it, but looking at the way in which Tiffany forced my son to describe it to the police officer was ridiculous.

She had him tell the officer that I punched him in the face with a closed fist. A six-foot-tall 210 lbs. man punching a four-year-old that couldn't have weighed more than fifty pounds at the time, with a closed fist in the face. I know that a fist in the face of a four-year-old would have produced a lot more than a small bruise on his face, it would have produced at a minimum a few missing teeth, and possibly a fractured jaw.

Now I know I wasn't Hercules, but I was strong enough to throw a good punch if I had to. That alone is proof that the story the child told wasn't true. If Tiffany was smart, and thank heaven she wasn't, she would have had our son say that I used my fingers to flick him in the face or had smacked him with an open hand. Anything would have sounded more realistic than a closed fist. Then there was the fact that my dad was with my son and I the entire time. My dad was always with us from the moment we picked him up, until the time we dropped him off to her.

We did this for multiple reasons. One was because my dad loved spending time with his grandson, and two, so that when she would falsely accuse me of something, I would always have a witness present to prove her lies to be what there were, lies. Add to this the third fact in this scenario, and that is that my son had his physical that same day. His doctor had checked him over, from head to toe, just two hours before my dad and I dropped him off to her. Tiffany's plan was not well thought out.

Some of you may be thinking, why would the child lie against the dad that treated him so well? Jonathan knew he was safe with me. He knew I would not beat him even if he told a lie about me. His mother, on the other hand, would threaten him to say the lies. If he didn't do what she said. Jonathan knew what punishment or cruelty awaited him.

The point of most concern here is the fact that Tiffany had her mother intentionally abuse my son, and that her husband, an officer of the Sheriff's office, was presumably involved, and aware of this. My son did not have a bruise on his face at the time of his physical, as was noted by his pediatrician in an affidavit filled out and signed by her that DCFS had obtained.

Nor did my son obtain a bruise in the approximate two hours of time between the doctor's appointment and the time Tiffany picked him up from the mall, as was verifiable by my dad, who was present, had anyone cared to ask him.

With all other options ruled out, it would appear as though it was my son's maternal grandmother that had abused him on this day, however, it theoretically could have also been his stepdad's mom.

We know that the abuse did occur because the police officer that responded to Tiffany's call had noted in his report that he did indeed see a small mark on my son's face. I believe he described it as a mark, not a bruise. Significance of this is that a bruise would imply that it was black and blue, or maybe a greenish color, as if it had happened much earlier than the time that it was reported, whereas a mark on his face, which I think the officer indicated was red colored, would indicate that it occurred recently.

As I write this, I wonder how a human being could do these things to a child. I know that things like this, and things much worse than this, happen to children all over the world, but I will never be able to understand why. I know we could get into the discussion of why God would allow this, and then we could discuss the topic of free will and leave it at that. My question is not why God allows this, but why do people choose to do these things.

Chapter Twenty-Six

Crooked Cops

I can't tell you this story without telling you about the police department's detective that oversaw the investigation of our case. Her name was Sally Thurman. I don't know how long she had worked for the department or what her story was. The only thing I know is that she was corrupt. I understand the need to thoroughly investigate all claims of child abuse to do the best you possibly can to protect our community's most vulnerable members. It makes sense to do a thorough investigation. I am all for detailed reports written and investigated with integrity.

It doesn't make sense to purposefully omit relevant facts and witnesses, as she did in my son's case. After being contacted by the police officer the morning after Tiffany filed her report, I was concerned and so I went to get a copy of the police report and saw that the officer noted seeing a mark on my son's face, I wanted to find out exactly how it happened and what was being done about it, if anything at all.

Typically, I would find out that nothing would be done about the abuse that my son endured. This time however, not only would nothing be done to his abuser, but they would try to prosecute me instead.

I had picked up the police report and asked to speak to the officer that had taken the report, and they directed me to detective Sally Thurman. They told me she was the one handling the case. I called her to ask her what was going on and what she was doing to try to protect my son, and I asked her if I could meet with her to further discuss this. I made an appointment to see her. When I arrived, I thought I was meeting her to ask her questions, as I had asked to meet her to discuss what was being done to protect my son. Instead, she shoved a piece of paper in front of me to sign, stating that I agree to talk to her without an attorney present, and consent to the recording of the meeting.

I did later obtain a copy of the meeting and still have it. As I tried to ask her what she planned on doing to protect my son, she went on to question me as if I had done something wrong. Ms. Thurman went on and on asking me how I spend my time with my son, and what I feed him each day, things that don't seem very relevant to the fact that my son was being physically abused, but I just answered the questions anyway. I remember telling her that he likes to go play at the playgrounds at the mall and Burger King and McDonalds. She seemed very concerned about the fact that I feed my four-year-old son Burger King and McDonalds, criticizing my choice to do so, acting as though it was a crime. Detective Thurman was very focused on his eating habits.

I don't remember the entire content of the meeting, other than that she was accusing me of hitting my son with a closed fist and leaving a mark on his face, as described in the police report. I questioned her about the fact that the report stated that my son told the officer that his grandmother had done it, and asked if she had brought his grandmother in for questioning, and she said, "No". I asked why, she couldn't answer. Detective Thurman didn't ask me what I was doing the day of the report being filed. So, I told her. I gave her an account of the entire day, accounting for every minute, from the physical at the pediatrician's office, to the mall, including the fact that my dad was with us the entire time. I told her to contact my dad to question him about the details of that day.

Ms. Thurman never did. Why? Because had she done so, she would have proof that the mark on my son's face hadn't occurred until after his mother picked him up. I then suggested that Detective Thurman contact the pediatrician's office to confirm the physical and find out from the pediatrician if there was any such bruise or marks on my son. She didn't. Why? Because if she did, she would have found out that at 4:00 PM on that Wednesday at the doctor's office, he had no such bruise or mark on him, proving once again that the coerced allegation from my four-year-old son was indeed false.

Why would she willfully fail to follow up on all leads, witnesses and evidence presented to her? Because if she did, it would prove that the child was so terrified of his mother, he would do or say anything to keep from getting beat, or burned, or any other sick things he knew his mother would do to him. He was easily coerced into making the false allegation, and it would lead her to the person that did abuse my son.

Jonathan shook when he had to go back to his mom's house. I only wish the videotapes of Jonathan's heart-breaking sobs, while he begged to not be sent back to his mother or grandmother would have been allowed to be shown in court as evidence. So many times, he was inconsolable when he had to go back to Tiffany. He never knew what his mother or grandmother might do to him. Plus, Tiffany was constantly creating drama, and was a very good actress. She played the part of a helpless victim well.

Why did the detective not want the truth? It was quickly becoming obvious. Any evidence gathered during an investigation, is not a public record during the investigation pursuant to Florida law. The video and audio recording of my meeting with Detective Sally Thurman were not allowed to be given to anyone not investigating the case according to the law. It would only be a few days after this meeting that Tiffany would begin questioning me about every meal and snack that our son ate while he was with me. This didn't begin before my meeting with Detective Sally Thurman, it began AFTER my meeting with Detective Sally Thurman. Was it a weird coincidence that during our meeting, Detective Sally Thurman was excessively focused on what I fed my son while he was with me, and then just days later Tiffany began questioning me about what I feed our son every day?

Tiffany would even use the whole "feeding him fast food" in her court documents just a couple of months later to try to change the custody agreement, alleging that feeding him fast food was a legal basis for a modification of custody. I'm not an idiot, and I could clearly see that despite the fact that it was illegal, Detective Sally Thurman had either given Tiffany a copy of the video or discussed our meeting with her and her husband in great length.

When I realized they were working together, I thought I was smart enough to catch them doing so. I knew the police department had security cameras in front of the building that could see every person that walked in and out of the front doors. Realizing that Tiffany had been to the Police department just days after my meeting with Detective Sally Thurman and that Detective Sally Thurman had most presumably, and illegally given Tiffany a copy of the video of my meeting with her, I thought I could obtain proof of Tiffany walking into the police department sometime after my meeting with Detective Sally Thurman.

About two weeks after my meeting, I requested a copy of the surveillance tapes for a period of seven days after my meeting with Thurman, just to be told by the police department that they only keep the tapes for twenty-four hours before erasing them. That is the most ridiculous thing I've ever heard.

During my time working with my income tax preparation company at several Walmart locations I found out that Walmart keeps their security camera footage for ninety days. That's right, Walmart keeps their security camera footage for ninety days, but the police department only keeps theirs for twenty-four hours. How convenient. After the case was closed, I would request phone records of any calls made by police department Detective Sally Thurman to any party about this case, which is, according to Florida law, public record once the case is closed. I received a report of probably forty or fifty calls made by Detective Sally Thurman during this investigation, and around fifteen to twenty of them were made to Tiffany's husband, Kaleb, investigative assistant at the sheriff's office. Some of them were as much as ten to fifteen minutes in length. All were made during an active investigation. I can't say for certain what was discussed during all these phone calls, but one could only assume.

What would make me so suspicious of detective Thurman's behavior, is that despite all the evidence that was available to her, including my son telling the officer that his grandmother had hurt him, she willfully refused to question his maternal grandmother, and willfully refused to interview my dad, who happened to be with my son the entire day that he was allegedly abused by me. I presented to Detective Sally Thurman a copy of my son's physical. Jonathan's pediatrician has absolutely no record of Detective Sally Thurman contacting their office, nor did she follow up with any leads or witnesses I meticulously provided for her.

She willfully failed to do any of this. Ms. Thurman then proceeded to send my file to the Florida State attorney's office requesting that they prosecute me for child abuse, stating in her report to them that I was guilty, as if it were a proven fact, which I'm sure constitutes a civil law violation of slander and liable, or defamation of character.

These documents are now public record, and having been a well-known individual in my community for so many years, these inaccurate statements and false allegations made against me could have had a significant impact against me and may have contributed to the loss of income, and the death of my character in the eyes of the people that trust me to manage their finances during the course of running my business.

I know I might be making a bigger deal about this than I should, but when a corrupt cop is trying to falsely imprison you, and trying to destroy your credibility, which, let's face it, has a dollar value attached to it, it can anger any person that has to deal with this.

I know the attorney that I consult with in regard to the publishing of this book will advise me to not use real names, and I will agree to this, for most of the people that I am writing about in this book. Why? Out of respect for them, whether that respect has been earned by them or not, and out of mercy. It is not my intent to shame anyone that I am writing about here in this book. Let's face it, they have already done that for themselves with the actions they have taken and the choices they have made. It is my belief that I should have mercy on those that have acted in a criminal, immoral, and unethical manner, which has unfortunately had a negative impact on my life and on the life of my son, having caused years of child abuse to be hidden and swept under the rug.

The abuser has been protected, time and time again, while the abused have gone unnoticed. However, those individuals that are in a position of power and authority, and misuse that power and authority for their own pleasure, and end up trying to falsely imprison people, and protect the guilty by looking the other way when a child is being hurt, those people must be stopped. I can't imagine how many people have spent years in prison or are still in prison today for a crime they didn't commit because of Sally Thurman's tainted reports, untrue statements and allegations. I hope that shedding light on her corruption will at least compel the current chief of the police and the department to do a thorough investigation into every case she worked that resulted in the imprisonment of the alleged suspect.

Considering she tried to have me falsely prosecuted, I'm sure there are many people who were falsely imprisoned that I believe deserve restitution for what happened to them. I also think about the corrupt counselor, Tina, that I'm sure has testified in many divorce and custody hearings that resulted in someone getting screwed over because of her lies, and children being wrongfully taken from parents that didn't deserve to lose them, because she lied about them. As I mentioned earlier, I know of at least one other guy that she screwed over, and she should have her licensed revoked before she destroys other innocent lives.

Chapter Twenty-Seven

Back in Court Again

The department of Children and Family Services were contacted by the police officer that had taken the initial report. This time there was a gentleman named William Hoffman that had been assigned to our case. He recognized this was a bunch of garbage and closed the case. He did do a thorough investigation though, unlike Detective Sally Thurman. He contacted Jonathan's pediatrician's office and spoke to the doctor. He had her fill out an affidavit describing my son's condition at the time of the physical. There weren't any bruises or marks on him when she completed the physical.

He didn't talk to the witness that was present at the time of the alleged incident occurred, my dad, but I assume that after he had spoken to the doctor, read the police report, and had considered that fact that Tiffany had indeed been stalking us by following us to our church, he had seen enough to know what this was.

Ultimately, the entire case was dropped. DCFS closed its investigation since it wasn't real. The States Attorney's office closed the case too. Her attempt to see me rot in jail for years failed. Sometimes people hate you for no good reason, other than they sense you have a covenant with God. They try to do all manner of maliciousness against you, but if you belong to God, you can be sure He's got your back. He has so many moves that the evil one can't even begin to imagine how God will annihilate him.

All of this came about because I requested a better, healthier day care. My attorney, Michael Anderson, sent Tiffany a letter with copies of all the administrative code violations and fines, and documentation indicating that the state of Florida, through the Department of Children and Family services, had closed the daycare that she had our son in. After receiving this she continued to refuse to remove our son from Kid Kingdom Daycare. Michael Anderson had to file a motion with the court requesting that the court remove our son from this daycare. Once again, I had to spend thousands of dollars to compel Tiffany to do what I requested and what any good parent would have done automatically.

Once again, I was in court in November 2007. We stood in front of Judge Lisa Nelson and explained the situation. My attorney requested in the court documents that the court order Tiffany to pay my legal expenses, which we thought was reasonable because her refusal to remove our son from this condemned daycare from hell was willful and defiant.

The court ultimately chose to correct the situation by requesting a list of three daycare providers from each of us so that it could select one at random. The court had chosen not to assert responsibility to the party at fault and chose not to hold her accountable by requiring reimbursement of legal fees. Big surprise, right? In 2007 the Florida courts were still very gender biased. The court ended up selecting a Christian daycare. At the time, I thought it was a great choice on the part of the court. This daycare facility had appeared to be well operated and managed.

At the time, I didn't understand that daycares operating under the umbrella of a religious organization were exempt from DCFS oversight. This simply meant that the daycare wasn't subjected to DCFS inspections as other daycares would be. It was only months after this that I hired a young lady to work at my office that had owned and operated a small daycare in the area and had also in the past been a DCFS investigator. This young lady, Kirsten, told me she had responded to reports of abuse at my son's new daycare. She told me that while the allegations couldn't be proven, she believed them to be true. So once again, my son was in a bad situation, and my hands were tied.

Just weeks after completing the daycare litigation, Tiffany, was cockier than ever. She filed a petition to modify custody. This time, her intent was to take more money from me. And after getting away with all that she did, the whole daycare thing, kidnapping and bogus restraining orders and contempt of court, Tiffany knew she had the power to do whatever she wanted whenever she wanted, and that the court wouldn't do anything about it.

In the state of Florida, the law requires a substantial change in circumstances to qualify for a change or modification of custody. While there wasn't any substantial change in circumstances, our previous custody agreement, had language in it allowing for a modification of time share schedule when our son reached school age. This was placed in the agreement to allow us to change the schedule to accommodate the loss of time with our son that would result from him starting school.

This round of litigation would last a little less than a year. As always, I would spend thousands and thousands of dollars for no reason, when any change of the time-sharing schedule could've been done between any two mentally stable and mature adults without the need for lawyers.

However, Tiffany wasn't either of those things. Tiffany had used her most recent vendetta, the coercing of my son to falsely accuse me, and the corrupt detective, to make it clear to me that I would have to continue to pay for my freedom, and pay I did. We ended up agreeing to an increase in timeshare for me, from

2.5 days a week, to 3 days a week, with an increase in the child support that I paid her, almost tripling it. I really didn't have a choice. If my son was her paycheck, and she was taking as much money from me as she possibly could, I was worth more to her alive and with my freedom, than dead or behind bars.

Dead people don't pay baby mamma support, and neither do people behind bars. I agreed to pay so that I could see my son, in a legal system that requires a dad to participate in a pay per visit program, kind of like the pay-per-view programs on TV. If you want to see your child, you pay per visit. Now before you begin to think, why is this man complaining about paying child support, please understand that the 'child support' money I paid her was never used for the benefit of my son, at least, not much of it, other than to provide him food for the four days a week he was with her.

I would buy all of Jonathan's clothes and shoes. I would send him to school in the morning with clothes that fit him, then when she would pick him up, she would keep them and send him to school the next day, or the day after, whichever day that I was scheduled to pick him up from school, with uniforms from the year before that didn't fit him. The shorts would be so tight that he would come home and show me the red marks that were around his waist from the tight shorts. The shirts would barely cover his stomach they were so short. Then in the winter, I would pick him up with pants that were so short that his socks would show. This was an ongoing issue for years, where she would keep and collect all the new clothes that I purchased for him, and dispose of his old stuff by sending him to my house with the stuff that didn't fit.

Even if she held a grudge against me, any parent that loved their child, would not want the child actually hurting his feet and waist with blisters because his shoes and waist band were so tight.

I paid directly for half of all his medical expenses, which weren't much, since she had him on Medicaid. I would find out several years later that she was committing welfare fraud, lying on her application for Medicaid and financial assistance, while her husband worked at the sheriff's office making around $50,000 plus each year. Tiffany and her husband would steal tens of thousands of dollars from the state of Florida throughout the years. I would end up always paying for all of his other expenses. So very little of the money that I gave her was used for his benefit. A small amount was used for his food. None of it was used for clothes, medical expenses, or anything else.

This round of litigation would end in the fall of 2008 and would be the last round until the big one. The final battle of this war wouldn't be fought for almost seven more years.

During these years between 2008 and 2015, we had our usual difficulties. Tiffany consistently refused to be civilized, nor would she ever cooperate. There would be times when I needed to ask her to switch days with me, with her taking our son on one of my days with him and letting me have one of her days with him in exchange. I would usually have to do this not more than two or three times a year for work. Most of the times that I asked it would become a battle. She would simply refuse for no reason, other than to create chaos.

There were some other memorable times during these years. One of which occurred in October 2008. This is when I had told my son about a medical issue I had with my eye, and how several days later, it had gotten better. To try to strengthen his faith, I told him that I had prayed for my eye to get better, and it did. I told him that God answered my prayer. He then looks at me with a look of confusion on his face. He then says, "God doesn't answer my prayers." Then I asked him what he meant. He said, "I pray to God asking Him to let me live with daddy forever." When I heard him say that, I was in shock. I knew things were bad for him while living with his mother several days a week, but to think that they were so bad that a five-year-old boy would pray to God to save him from the misery was absolutely unbelievable. It hurt my heart to hear him say that. He had been praying for a miracle, at such a young age, and was confused as to why God didn't hear his prayers. I tried to explain to him that sometimes God doesn't answer our prayers right away, but that I believe that someday He will. I had not told Jonathan about God's promise at this time. He was simply too young for something like that.

Then there was the time I took Jonathan on a weekend cruise in August 2010. You would think that going on a weekend getaway would not be something that would create the World War III type of conflict. But with Tiffany, it did. Something so simple, would be turned into such chaos. The chaos she created over this was absolutely insane. I had taken Jonathan on this cruise on a weekend that I had him, so it wasn't interfering with her parenting time. There really wasn't any reason to make a fuss about it at all. I informed her via email that Jonathan would be on a cruise with me for the weekend. Our court order required that we each keep the other party aware of our son's well-being and whereabouts when requested by the other party, or any other time that it was relevant. I felt that taking Jonathan to the Bahamas was an occasion that would require that I notify her of his whereabouts. So out of an abundance of caution, I informed her in advance. I wanted to make sure I was complying with our court order as I always had done. So, I fulfilled my obligation to inform her.

My phone didn't have cellular service while in the Bahamas. When we arrived at one of the islands, we found a McDonalds that had Wi-Fi. I had Jonathan call her through an app on our phone that made phone calls via the internet.

For some reason unknown to Jonathan or myself, she was furious that we went on a cruise, and went absolutely ballistic, sending harassing emails, texts, and voice messages on my phone. She was threatening to call her lawyer, call the police, and report the fact that I went on a cruise with our son.

After receiving some of her threatening and harassing messages on my phone while we were connected to the Wi-Fi on the island, my son and I both became very stressed and anxious about the chaos she was creating. It really ruined our weekend.

When we arrived back in Florida and got off the ship, my cellular service was active again, and oh my goodness, there were many more threatening messages popping up in my email, text messages and voicemail. Tiffany had actually called the police while we were on the cruise. I had a voice message on my phone from a police officer, telling me that he received a report from Tiffany that I had taken our son on a cruise, and he was following up on the report. He said that he had stopped by my house and seen that no one was home. He was giggling while he was leaving the message, saying that he was sorry to have to bother me, but he had to follow up. He ended the message by saying that he hopes we enjoy our cruise, and that he was so sorry for bothering me. It was kind of hilarious that she would call the police to report that her child's father went on a cruise, as if it were a crime. Based on the voicemail that the officer left, I can tell that he knew that she was insane. He left his cell phone number, so I called him back. I talked to him for a minute to let him know I had just received his message, and we both had a laugh about it, and then I let him get back to work. Now while it seemed funny at the moment, it really wasn't. When we got off the ship, I dialed her number to let Jonathan say hi to her, and she started yelling and screaming, telling him to put me on the phone, and then continued screaming for no reason. She was yelling, "You think you're invincible, you think you're invincible." I didn't say a word, and after listening for a moment, I politely said, "I got to go", and hung up the phone. Jonathan heard the screaming, and it frightened him even more. It frightened him so much, that when we arrived home, he vomited all over the bathroom floor. The fear had made him sick to his stomach. He told me that he was afraid and didn't want to go back to his mother's house.

Having to live through this, day after day, week after week, month after month, and year after year, was probably the most difficult thing I had to do in my life. I had to stand there and watch my son be so afraid that it made him physically sick. I couldn't imagine what was waiting for him when he went back to her. There was no way to have known that going on a weekend cruise would send her into a rage. No one had done anything wrong. It was impossible to have foreseen that she would cause so much destruction over absolutely nothing.

I will never forget that day that we came home from the cruise, and I had to send him to school, knowing that just hours later, he would once again be back in the hands of the beast. It broke my heart having to see him living in such fear. It hurt so much to have to send him back, as it did almost every time I had to do it, for thirteen and a half years. A child shouldn't have to live their life in constant fear.

These were just a few of the painful and heartbreaking incidences that occurred throughout the years between 2008 and 2015. There were so many more, but too many to mention.

Chapter Twenty-Eight

Our Forever Home

Fast forwarding to the spring of 2015, many years had passed, and we were still living under the same set of circumstances. Very little had changed, but the time for God's promise to be fulfilled was drawing near. It was in 2012 that God had told me when it would begin, and I remember making a post on Facebook at this time, referencing the time frame in which it would come to pass. It would begin in the late summer of 2015.

Early in 2015 I became so excited knowing that we were so close. Several times in the spring and summer of 2015 I excitedly told Jonathan what God had promised, and that it was coming soon. One night just after he laid down to go to sleep, we began our prayers. After we finished, I told him that he would be coming home to live with me, and that he would not have to go back to his mom's house. I promised Jonathan a forever home that he would never have to leave again.

I had no fear or concerns about sharing God's promises with him, because I knew it was guaranteed by God. I knew that I could share with Jonathan God's precious promises, and that he would never be disappointed.

He would ask me how I knew, and I would tell him that God told me. I can't imagine how difficult it could be for a child to try to understand this, how an invisible God could be so present in our visible world. It's still amazing to think that because of the fulfillment of this promise, my son saw the glory of God. He witnessed God's glory first hand. It's difficult enough for me as an adult to wrap my mind around the fact that the Creator of universe would reveal Himself to me. He promised me things that the world would describe as impossible. Yet with God nothing is impossible.

God gave me the faith and confidence to believe His every promise was going to happen no matter how unattainable it looked. Why did He tell me three years in advance exactly when it would begin? Because He loves us so much. It's breathtaking! This experience, as well as many others, has given me the ability to believe in the impossible, it has given me the ability to know that in an instant everything that is wrong in your life, can become right!

I wondered why He would tease me with such a promise so soon, and then to have to suffer through so many years before it was fulfilled. In my reasoning it seemed senseless to have to wait so long. My life and the life of my son would have been so much better had He done it sooner.

In the book of Ecclesiastes chapter 3 verse 1, it says *"There is an appointed time for everything. And there is a time for every event under the heavens."*

This scripture can be used as a reminder that just because what we are hoping for isn't happening right now, it doesn't mean that it's never going to happen. It has taught me patience and tenacity. Never give up, no matter what!

I am also puzzled why God would even promise me anything at all. Why not just do it? Why all the hype of promising me something if you had no intention of giving it to me for another thirteen and a half years? All this would do is frustrate me. The waiting would seem like torture. Could there have been a purpose in doing so?

The book of John chapter 13 verse 19 states: *"I am telling you now before it happens, so that when it does happen, you will believe that I am who I am."*

This scripture tells it all. If God had not promised me in March 2003 that He would someday bring my baby home, and just did it, it probably would not have been evident to me that it was indeed God that had done it. I might have assumed that if it ever did happen, that it was done by my efforts, and my strength alone.

Without God's intervention, it would have never happened. I was told by numerous attorneys, for many years, that something of this nature could not be done, especially when Jonathan was just thirteen and a half years old. My son was scared to death of his mother. He had been abused for so many years and had lived in fear his whole life. I was told by several people who had suffered abuse as a child, that based upon their own experience, he wouldn't be strong enough to stand against Tiffany until he was at least sixteen years old.

One of my friends had run away from his home, and away from his abusive stepfather at the age of sixteen. My dad stood face to face with his abusive father for the first time when he was sixteen years old. At thirteen and a half years old, Jonathan was simply not equipped to be able to stand against her. The only way would be for my son's mother to have walked away of her own free will. The court records document that she would fight relentlessly for years and years to maintain power and control over her victims.

Not having control was simply not an option for her. The absence of power and control in her adult life was very traumatizing for Tiffany. It would understandably bring her back in her mind to the horrific experiences that she endured for years as a child, in situations where she had no power or control. My son and I had to pay for the sins of her father. There was simply no way that she would ever surrender. My attorney Mr. Anderson had pointed to this fact many times. He would reference the ten plus years of litigation that had accumulated. His wisdom and experience had painted the picture that he could see. Tiffany's relentless pursuit of chaos and destruction appeared to have no end. And he was right. At least as far as the evidence indicated.

So as the book of John 13:19 states, telling me what would happen before it happened would be evidence that it is He that promised it, and that it was He that delivered.

I believe the waiting was for building faith, hope, and a dependence on Him which would ultimately lead to a relationship with Him that would transcend all the difficulties of this world.

As the appointed time began to approach, I began to speculate how it would all begin to transpire. There was no major conflict at the time. I honestly couldn't see the spark that would ignite the flame. There were some issues that arose in the summer of 2015, but nothing that would draw a clear path to God's promise. We had a disagreement about sending our son to church summer camp for a week. He wanted to go, but she was adamantly opposed because of its religious affiliation. I talked to my attorney, Mr. Anderson, about how we could persuade her to agree to what our son desired, and what was best for him. He reminded me that the law doesn't require her to be cooperative, logical, and civilized. He stated that a one-week camping trip isn't anything that a court would care about, and we simply couldn't do anything about it.

Another issue that arose in the early summer of 2015 was that my son wanted to enter a talent competition that was scheduled to take place on a day that he was with me, and she fought tooth and nail to prevent him from going. Why? Simply because it was a church sponsored talent competition. Tiffany honestly had no right to try to interfere, as it was not her designated day to care for our son, and I had the right to take him to a talent competition if I so desired.

One other memorable conflict that arose around this time was the fact that after several years of sharing our son's Christmas vacation from school, she suddenly refused to do so in December 2014. We each would have him for a week during Christmas vacation every year since around 2006 and I would always take him on a road trip up north to let him see the snow.

Being a Florida boy, he never had the privilege of making a snowman, or throwing a snowball at his dad, or simply enjoying the experience of playing in the snow. I tried to give him that experience for a week every year. He really enjoyed it. We weren't always lucky enough to have a white Christmas every year that we traveled up north, but most times we did. We had gone to places like Tennessee, Massachusetts, New York City, Washington DC with the hopes of getting some snow while we were there.

The first time Jonathan saw snow was in December 2006 and he was just about to turn four years old. I took him to Illinois to see my sister and her family for the holiday season. We had our bed in the basement. When I awakened and went upstairs, I saw that there was a blizzard outside. There was about two feet of snow, and it was still falling from the sky. My sister had a huge window in the living room where you could get a beautiful view of the winter wonderland that was being created outside. I immediately went downstairs to wake Jonathan up, and we both ran up the stairs to the kitchen, then ran around to the living room where he saw snow for the first time Jonathan was so excited. He was in his pajamas and wanted to run outside right away to play.

I explained to him that we needed a coat, hat, gloves and boots on him before we went outside because it was so cold. After getting all wrapped up in winter clothes, we went outside, and he had such a comical time with his cousin and snow buddy, Mark.

They pelted each other with snow, laughing so hard they kept sliding off their feet. Both boys completely ignored the freezing temperatures. Mark and Jonathan threw snowballs at each other and with fiendish delight ganged up on me and rapidly hit me from every angle possible. In fact, anything that didn't move, was hit with snow. I loved seeing Jonathan have the time of his life. God knew my young son needed all the laughter he could get.

For Tiffany it was always about control. These and countless other small power struggles that she created, made life so difficult. None of the struggles were anything that would rise to the level of a parent losing all parental rights, allowing for God's promise to be fulfilled in having my son come home.

As history had indicated, kidnapping, child abuse, stalking, harassment, threats, false accusations, and attempted murder weren't enough either. Half of the things that Tiffany did throughout the years simply weren't provable to a standard that would allow for losing her son, and the other half of the atrocities committed by her throughout the years were either swept under the rug by her husband and his connections that he had while working at the Sheriff's office, or it was simply ignored by the authorities.

After having been through all that we had been through with no results, it was difficult to imagine how this could be done. Any man that had been though all of this would have lost all hope, had it not been for the promise of God. I realize that based on the circumstances, it was me that should have been the one to surrender. Just as I knew the sun would rise in the morning, I knew that Jonathan was coming home.

One night in the middle of the summer of 2015, Erica and I sat on the couch for hours discussing the possible scenarios that could begin the process. After having suffered for so many years, I knew there would be a price to pay for what was to come. It would not come easy and it wouldn't be cheap. While I was sure His promise would come to pass, there was never any promise made to me that there wouldn't be casualties along the way. As the weeks began to pass, I would consult with Erica and my family to try to design a plan that would keep us all as safe as possible because I knew the process would soon begin.

Before this battle would begin, I went to Best Buy to purchase security cameras to place around the perimeter of my house. I already had an alarm system on my home for many years, so we were good there. With the cameras and alarm system, Erica and I felt as though the house was as secure as it could possibly be. I also alerted the neighbors to the potential issues and asked them to pay attention to anything that seemed to be out of the ordinary.

My mom and I both have a Florida concealed weapons permit and we both have handguns. My dad decided to get his Florida concealed weapons permit also, as well as a handgun in the summer of 2015. We were all as well prepared as we could be for the worst-case scenario. With her having done both physically aggressive criminal acts in the past, and because she manipulated the legal system with lies, false accusations and the coercion of my son to falsely accuse me, we simply didn't know what direction she'd take this time.

History has proven that we could be sure of at least two things. First, that Tiffany was dangerous and that my life and my freedom could once again be in danger. Second, is that when litigation begins, it is a guarantee that things are going to get out of hand real fast. While we had done all that we could to prepare ourselves, all we could do next was wait. The time frame that I was made aware of several years earlier was the end of July 2015.

I thought the process would begin on its own, without any action to be taken on my part. July 2015 had rolled around, and nothing happened. Then it was August, and still nothing. As the weeks continued to pass with nothing happening, it became increasingly obvious that I would have to do something to get the ball rolling.

We were still facing the petty issues of Tiffany refusing to allow our son to go to a summer camp, the annual sharing of his Christmas vacation from school, as well as refusing to switch days for work, and various other small issues.

I thought it would be a great time to modify our custody agreement to include provisions for these things. It was approximately August 2015 that I sent her an email asking her to meet with me and a mediator to discuss some possible changes to our custody agreement. Our existing custody agreement required that we meet with a mediator prior to beginning litigation.

As was her tradition of violating the court's order, Tiffany chose to refuse to even communicate with me at all concerning some minor changes that I was looking to make. Instead of communicating with me, and meeting with a mediator, she chose to violate our court order and file a petition to modify our custody agreement. All because I asked her to communicate with me about some minor changes that I wanted to discuss.

My son and I were on our ten-day court ordered summer vacation in New York City when I sent Tiffany the email requesting that we meet. I decided that I would need to tell my son that I emailed her this request so he could be aware of what was happening. I wanted him to be aware, so he wasn't caught off guard when he went back to his mother's home and was interrogated by her about it.

Jonathan certainly knew what to expect, and he was scared to death. He was very upset that I had emailed his mother this request. He knew the price he would have to pay when he was back at her house.

Jonathan knew the living hell he would have to go through as a result, and he was scared. I ached for him because I knew the suffering he would endure, and also the fear, and anxiety. It was a difficult decision for me to make. It hurt a lot, knowing that my choice would place him in a very bad position. It felt like I was betraying him, and I was afraid that he would see it that way as well. He knew we always had to be quiet and give her everything she wanted in order to keep the peace. As any young child trying to survive in a home with violence and abuse, he would simply try to fly under the radar. Jonathan kept his mouth shut, told her what she wanted to hear when she asked him, and stayed out of her way, hoping that she might not notice him enough to unleash her fury on him every day.

We were at Madison Square Garden, about to take a tour when I told him about the email I had to send. The rest of the day would be ruined for him. I could see the effort he made to mask the anxiety and fear with the entertainment we were partaking in. All day I could see the anxiety on his face, indicating that the wheels in his head were spinning. He was dreading what would happen when he had to go back, most presumably trying to think of a way to survive and trying to think of a way he would be able to endure his mom's wrath.

This was a lot to ask of a twelve-year-old boy. I was basically asking him to put himself on the line in favor of a promise that a God he couldn't see, and a God that he couldn't hear, had made to me.

Of course, I would wonder, what if I was wrong? What if I misunderstood what I believed God had told me? What if it wasn't God? What if it was the devil that had told me this, with a plan of deceiving me into a trap that would ultimately consume us all? Our lives were literally at stake, with the realistic possibility that she would hurt him greater than she ever had before, and that she would once again attempt to take my life, with the possibility of being successful this time around. My freedom and my everything were at stake. I gambled it all on a promise that God had made twelve and a half years earlier.

If you want to call me crazy for having done so, I wouldn't be offended. Because the truth is, no man in his right mind would have dared to awaken the beast. It's like going into the battle of Armageddon, facing the rage and fury of the beast, not knowing if you are alone, in which case the beast would most certainly devour you, or if God, the Creator of the universe, was with you. It was kind of like the story of David and Goliath. This young shepherd boy wasn't prepared to go to battle against a giant. He went to battle with a monster that should have destroyed him. He did so because he had the assurance that God was with him. If he had been wrong about the plan that God had for him, he would have lost his life.

This was the choice I had made for myself, to surrender my life to the God that I trusted, to the God that I knew would see us through the battle. But for me to impose my faith and my trust in

God onto a helpless child, a child that would not be able to protect himself, to a child that was not yet strong enough to face his giant, was one of the most difficult things I had to do. I knew he couldn't protect himself from the beast, and neither could I, but I knew that God could.

I did just as Abraham did when he placed his son Isaac on the altar to sacrifice to God. But just like with Abraham, God didn't desire his son's sacrifice, He desired Abraham's willingness to do so. He desired Abraham's commitment to surrender himself and all that he had to the God of all the universe. Complete surrender is what God required of Abraham. It was that complete surrender Abraham had made, that allowed God to work in his life and to accomplish all the glorious things that He accomplished through Abraham.

Just like Abraham, I had to have the willingness to surrender my life to Him. I had to have the obedience to surrender my son to Him. I did what so few parents could do, and I threw my child out to the lions. I trusted God to protect him, and I did so because I believed that He would not only protect him, but that He would also set him free *(John 8:36)*. It was because of my choice to do so, that I was able to see the glory of God work in my life and the life of my son as He carried us through the fire and delivered us from this evil.

Chapter Twenty-Nine

Never Surrender

Several days after sending Tiffany the email that would shake the foundation of our lives, we arrived safely back at home in Florida. At this point, I had only sent Jonathan's mom the email asking her to meet with me. She responded to my request, stating that she would not meet with me. A few days after coming home from our trip to New York, I was served with the court papers to modify the custody agreement. In the petition, she had requested primary custody, allowing me visitation only on every other weekend. This would be an enormous change in our parenting agreement if it was accomplished by Tiffany. We currently had a schedule that allowed her four days a week with our son and offered me three days a week.

What Tiffany was asking the court for essentially, was an average of one day a week for me. Not only was she asking for more time, but she was asking for more money. Tiffany had no basis to justify these requests, so of course, she would have to come up with some lies. The first and most concerning false allegation she made, in writing on the petition, was that I allegedly touched and rubbed our son in inappropriate and private places.

This is what she had threatened to do for years. Tiffany was prepared to do whatever it took to destroy me. I'm sure that her initial intent was to use this false allegation to scare me into surrendering to her, meaning, give her all the money that she was demanding and give my son to her. I don't believe her initial intent included carrying out this accusation all the way through to the end. It would take a lot of guts to carry this through till the end. She would have to once again coerce Jonathan to lie, which, at this time, we were all concerned that she could do. At twelve years old he was still scared of her.

With the task of having to coerce my son to lie against me, Tiffany faced the possibility that it would backfire on her and he would rat her out. While he was too young when this battle started, Jonathan wasn't when it finished. You see, the courts generally move very slow. And there are ways to slow down the process yourself. The longer it dragged out, the older he was becoming.

Tiffany was racing against the clock, and the little hand was quickly approaching midnight. The allegation, and the language in which it was written, allowed it to be interpreted in one of two distinctly different ways. First, it could be referring to the physical location that my son was located at during the times that she alleges I had touched Jonathan or rubbed him. In other words, she could have been implying that I had, for example, patted him on the shoulder while at the mall, embarrassing him in public, therefore being inappropriate. Or, Tiffany could have tried to imply that I had patted him on the shoulders while at home, aka a "private" location.

The other way the allegation could have been interpreted is as if I had been touching or rubbing him in private and inappropriate spots on his body. The way this allegation was made allowed for Tiffany to use it in either way she wanted to, when needed. It was quite smart, leaving herself an open door to go through if she felt the need. I can tell you that while she is one of the most mentally unstable and dangerous humans that I have ever known, Tiffany is also as dumb as a door knob, this idea typically would've come from her mother, but she had already passed.

After having read through a ton of literature that her husband had written, and I will explain that later, I could tell that while he too suffered from mental illness, including severe depression. He was actually very intelligent, but in an evil manipulative kind of way. I would have to assume that he had been the one to come up with this idea.

There were many other false accusations made in this court document, but this was the one that stood out the most of course because of the damage that could've been done if Tiffany had gone through with it.

The next allegation that Tiffany made is an interesting one. This one had some partial truth to it, although of course she twisted it up a bit and shaped it into something that it was not. She had alleged that one of the reasons that she believed justified a substantial change in custody was that I had told our son that I speak to a higher power, and that this higher power and I converse back and forth and this so-called "higher power" tells me things and that I tell Jonathan that I can predict when people will die and that this was disturbing to our son and was causing him emotional trauma.

First, Tiffany refers to something called a higher power. I don't know anyone by that title. I suppose God is indeed a power higher than us, but I believe it was her intent to abstain from using His name because she doesn't "believe" in God. Then again, I'm not sure if it's her disbelief in the existence of God or if she simply hates Him. When He didn't grant her wish to save her mom from cancer and when He didn't save her from years of childhood abuse, rather than try to get to know God better and establishing a relationship with Him, she decided that it would simply be easier to just hate Him. Typically, when a person feels as though God has let them down, they usually ask themselves, if God exists, why would He allow such things to happen?

The allegation refers to who I know as God, and it also refers to what we call prayer. Prayer, of course, is simply when someone communicates with God, usually presenting requests, and offering praise and thanksgiving for all He has done in our lives.

All of this is what she referred to as conversing with a higher power. Ok. I suppose a person could choose to describe it in that manner if they so desired. It was in some part an attack against the faith of my son and me, but that's fine. Christians have been persecuted for twenty centuries, and I don't suppose it's going to stop anytime soon.

According to Tiffany's allegation, believing in God and praying to Him was traumatic for our son and was, in her opinion, a basis for ending my parental rights. What she went on to allege in her petition, is that this higher power tells me when people are going to die and other garbage.

I suppose Tiffany was alleging that I was a psychic, or a fortune teller. Or maybe she was alleging that I was in some way involved in some supernatural activity, like witchcraft. People with borderline personality disorder have a characteristic where they project their own faults and behaviors onto others, by accusing others of doing what it is that they themselves are guilty of doing. This was no different. It was Tiffany and her husband that were involved in all manner of things dark, such as voodoo, witchcraft, psychic mediums and seances.

Tiffany and her husband worked with an occult practitioner to do what's referred to as a past life regression, where the psychic sits with you and helps find out what you were in your past life. Like if you were a fish in your past life, or maybe a cow, or a dragon, or maybe even a unicorn. Well, Tiffany and her husband were deeply involved in the occult, and this is the reason why she was accusing me of such things.

My son even told me of a time where Tiffany made him sit with her in some sort of seance like practice. She would require him to sit on the floor with her, meditating, and imagining, or envisioning a man sitting there with them. She would instruct him to join her in the worshipping of this spirit guide, which she forced him to do against his will. He didn't want to participate.

Deuteronomy 7:26 Warns of even just having idols in your home, such as Buddhas, good luck charms, astrology charts, horoscopes, etc.... It says that anyone having occult items will be cursed. If you do have these items, or any objects to do black or white magic, Ouija boards, video games using magic, etc., it can bring a curse even on little children.

If you have any of these items in your home, get rid of them! The Bible also forbids communicating with the dead. It tells us that evil spirits will masquerade as deceased loved ones. That is why when people go to psychics, they may know things only you or your relatives may know. Don't fall for it! Jesus said we would know people by their fruit. If someone's fruit is evil and crooked, then you know they are not from God. Ask God to forgive you and to cleanse your home of all evil. Some scriptures you might want to look up that deal with this are: Leviticus 19:26-31; Deuteronomy 18:10-12; Isaiah 47:10-14. I sure don't want God angry with me, or evil spirits having access to me or my family.

Tiffany and her husband were deeply involved in the occult. Tiffany even admitted in the deposition that she talks to dead people. Talking to the dead is called necromancy. It is forbidden in the Bible because it is essentially inviting an evil spirit to come. When we disobey what God has written in His Word, it opens us up for all kinds of evil to enter our lives. I don't know if that's funny or scary. I'll let you decide. I'm telling you, this is stuff that I couldn't make up if I tried. It is all available in writing, under oath, as recorded by a stenographer.

The only vague connection to the truth that Tiffany's allegation had, was the fact that God did indeed promise me that someday He would bring my son home. I was so excited because I knew the time was coming soon. I couldn't help but tell Jonathan many times what was promised to happen, before it happened. I know that telling him in advance, and then actually seeing it come to pass in his life, would allow him to see God as he had never seen Him before, and as most people never do.

I'm honestly not sure if Jonathan told Tiffany about this promise from God. I'm assuming he had to. Tiffany had to have some basis from which to build this allegation on. The interesting thing is that she very well could have known about the promise when she walked herself right into this final round of litigation.

Tiffany probably began this fight thinking that she could prove me wrong. Maybe she thought that by proving this "promise from God" to be make-believe, she could disprove the actual existence of God. She had worked hard over the years to try to brainwash our son Jonathan into believing there was no God. I must admit, going around proclaiming to everyone around me for years and years that someday God was going to bring my son home was quite a huge risk.

Had I been wrong, it would've made me out to be a fool, and I could've damaged Jonathan's faith in God by telling him that God was going to do something that potentially would not have happened if I were wrong. If Jonathan did tell her this, her actions were just a bold and arrogant display of defiance against

God. If he didn't tell her, and she didn't know, then the devil, unknowingly walked her right into God's plan for our lives.

Now I'm not going to lie to you. When I received these court documents, I was nervous. Although I already knew the ending, I couldn't see how I could possibly get there. In the natural, there simply was no path that would lead to victory. I had gone to my church's youth pastor and his wife one night after service to explain to them what my son and I were about to go through.

At the time, Jonathan had been performing in the youth band that was led by the youth pastor's wife. She worked with him one to two times a week in band practice and on-stage during Wednesday night services. I knew that not only would we need their prayers, but we would also need their support. I can't even imagine what life was like for him during these eighteen months. Towards the end, Jonathan began opening a little and told me about some of the chaos that had been occurring at his mom's house. I knew he wasn't telling me everything though. What child could? The fear that his mother would find out that he talked about what went on in his mom's home was terrifying!

I confided in our youth pastor and his wife about the false allegations that were implying sexual abuse. I told them a little bit of the history of the situation so they could understand the severity of the situation. They told me they would give my Jonathan a little more attention and would pray for us. We were beginning a battle that could have been devastating to our lives had it not worked out as promised. There were times that I felt like taking matters into my own hands and felt like doing what I had to do to ensure victory. I could have easily stooped to her level of criminal behavior, lies and false accusations. But I knew God's promise would never be fulfilled like that.

If God was going to do this, it wouldn't be by using the tactics of the devil. When things became difficult, He would remind me of His Word, where He says in Zechariah 4:6, "Not by might nor by power, but by my Spirit, says the Lord Almighty". He reminded me of this scripture on October 17, 2016. On this same day, I posted on my Facebook page this scripture, along with this bold declaration:

"The enemy will surrender, not because I fought and won, but because God has promised, and what He has promised, no one can stop, not even all the forces of darkness. Satan himself, will surrender. Not to me, not to my "might or power", but to His Spirit."

I knew I didn't have to do anything other than to surrender to Him. I knew He would take care of it all. When God wants our surrender, He also expects our obedience to the promptings He is guiding us with. Now don't get me wrong, I worked hard those eighteen months preparing for his mother's deposition in July 2016, and preparing for trial, had we gone that far. I spent at least a hundred hours or more organizing every document and planning out every strategy and preparing for every challenge that might come before me.

Now one of the first steps in family law litigation, such as divorce or child custody lawsuits is to provide the opposing party copies of all your financial documents. You must spend hours, and even days, gathering three years' worth of bank statements, credit card statements, pay stubs, tax returns and anything else they demanded. This would include copies of your health insurance cards, driver's license, passport and almost anything else that you could imagine.

I spent about a week downloading all these documents, printing them out, blacking out the account numbers on hundreds and hundreds of pages of documents. Sounds like fun doesn't it? It was monotonous, hard work and discomforting. Perfect strangers have access to the most personal details of your life. To give an account of your whole financial and personal life is discomforting. You also must obtain copies of every loan application you ever filled out, for your house, your car, for anything and everything. So after submitting all those documents to Tiffany, she had her attorney send my lawyer a letter requesting copies of checking account statements for a business account at Wells Fargo for the corporation that I was contracted to manage at the time. In the letter, the attorney even specifically requested bank statements for account number ending in #2902.

First, neither I nor my attorney complied with this request, as the Florida state law only requires you to present personal financial records and records of businesses in which you are a shareholder. I had not been a shareholder at the time of this litigation. The second thing of concern was how in the world she knew the corporation that I had worked for had a checking account at Wells Fargo, and how did Tiffany know what the account number was. She had never been given the account number by me, or by my attorney, but somehow, she had obtained the account number.

The only way I could imagine her being able to do this, is by having her husband obtain it illegally through the Sheriff's office that he was employed with. I was irritated about the total lack of privacy, and that a corrupt officer, her husband, had most presumably obtained financial records for her illegally. This was very frustrating. And as I am writing this, I'm remembering the fact that she had done this before in a 2007-2008 litigation, where she had somehow obtained a copy of my mortgage application before getting it through the legal process.

Now when it came time for her to present the same documents to my attorney, she very carefully omitted such things as her car loan application, and her mortgage application on the new house that her and her husband had just purchased a few months earlier. She also forgot credit card statements for several accounts that appeared on her checking account statements, as well as many other financial documents that were required. Tiffany obviously omitted certain documents in order to cover up some details about her finances, such as how her and her husband came up with $100,000 - $120,000 cash to use as a down payment on a new house that Tiffany and her husband purchased just a couple of years after filing bankruptcy. Also, Tiffany submitted a financial affidavit where she claimed to have absolutely no income at all, other than her husband's income of $50,000 a year while working at the sheriff's office.

There were a lot of things that she was hiding. Obviously, if Tiffany could have hidden all her income and assets, and had she maintained partial custody or won full custody of our son, she would be able to acquire more of my earnings. Tiffany had hundreds of thousands of dollars that she was hiding. My son told me that her and her husband had just started attending an online college that costs $35,000 a year, for each of them. They bought almost $20,000 worth of new TV's, furniture and electronics for their new $200,000 house.

All of this and so much more, was aquired on an officer's $50,000 annual gross salary. As Ricky Ricardo would say on the "I Love Lucy show": "Lucy, you've got some splaining to do". Not only were they paying cash for houses, and paying for all of this other stuff, they were also illegally obtaining welfare benefits from the State of Florida. I could only prove that they were obtaining Medicaid health insurance illegally, which is welfare fraud. I can only assume they might have been getting food stamps and other benefits from Florida taxpayers illegally as well. All of this, while being a police officer.

The next step in all family law lawsuits is taking part in mediation. The state of Florida requires you attend mediation prior to moving forward towards trial. Our previous court ordered agreement also required this before any new litigation was started, but she refused to honor the past agreement and caused much more expense. It was completely unnecessary. If Tiffany was mentally stable, she would have been able to communicate and compromise to provide the best and most loving environment for our son. Tiffany couldn't do that, all that her mental illness would allow her to do was to create chaos, pain and destruction. She would literally leave a path of destruction everywhere she went.

Tiffany was like a hurricane, passing through your life and tearing apart everything that is valuable to you. I'm not the only one she tried to destroy. Public records can tell you of other men that she filed bogus restraining orders against.

There were many male victims that she was obsessed with and would falsely accuse. There was one man specifically, Donald Lewis, a man that she stalked, harassed and tormented for years while she was in high school.

This poor guy was a few years older than her. They worked together at a fast-food restaurant when she was a teen. She was infatuated with him, but from what he told me, the feeling was never mutual.

While Tiffany and I were together, I found newspaper clippings of him and other memorabilia about him hidden in shoe boxes in our closet. I talked to him in 2003, just after we ended our relationship, and the first thing he said after I mentioned

Tiffany's name to him, was "I hoped I would never hear that name again in my life." He told me about how she would stalk him and would go around telling people he was her boyfriend. According to him he never was. Tiffany had hounded him and was relentless in her pursuit.

I contacted him to try to find out if he might be able to help me because of his experience with Tiffany. I hoped that he had some advice, some survival tips. He was smart enough to stay away from her. That was the only way to survive. I was a complete idiot. We were in a relationship for two years. I was engaged to Tiffany and had a child with her. There was clearly no way out of this. I would end up paying a heavy price for my foolishness. While he was smarter than I was, he still had to deal with the memory of pain and suffering.

When Tiffany found out I had talked to him, she became angry at him and called him, threatening to falsely accuse him of raping her. He called me up and told me what she had threatened to do to him and told me he had his mom contact their attorney to deal with the matter. I don't believe she pursued the false accusation but threatening to make it was bad enough. I was clearly not the only victim, but I was the one that couldn't escape.

Our attorneys scheduled our mandatory mediation meeting sometime in late 2015. We all met at the courthouse. We each had our separate meeting rooms, each with our attorneys. The mediator would go back and forth to communicate the other persons demands, requests, and comments. Now this meeting didn't last long. Shortly after taking our seats, the mediator came in and did her two-minute presentation to describe how the process works, and then she asked us for a brief summary of the case. My attorney presented to her an outline of what was going on.

She went over to Tiffany's meeting room to have the same discussion with her and began by gathering her requests and demands to take back and present to us. When she returned to our meeting room, she told us that Tiffany had stated to her that she was insisting upon receiving full custody, and she would grant me visitation an average of one day a week, which would have been down from 3 days a week.

Tiffany was demanding more money, double what I was already paying her in order to see my son. After the mediator finished speaking, I smiled and said, "That will never happen in this lifetime. It looks like we are done here." I proceeded to rise from my seat, gathering up my paper work and my briefcase, and my attorney, said, "Well, OK. It looks like we're done."

As we begin to make our way towards the door, the mediator politely thanked us for our time, and advised us that she would communicate to the other party that we were finished. I know for certain that Tiffany was not expecting this. Tiffany thought for sure that I would have caved in at the threat of false accusations of child molestation. She was certain that I would be scared and would surrender.

The confidence I had was so amazing. It was a gift from God. I was facing threats of allegations that could have landed me in prison for twenty-plus years and could have left my son in the hands of his greatest fear.

Despite all this, I was able to stand in assurance and walk away, knowing that this would not be the end of me. Knowing that you could walk through a fire and not be burned was one of the greatest feelings in the world. I knew in this one situation, that I was unstoppable. I knew that I was invincible, and that I could leap tall buildings with a single bound and run faster than a locomotive. Now wait a minute, that last part was Superman.

That's what he could do, leap tall buildings in a single bound, and he was more powerful than a locomotive. That's what the comic books said about Superman. But that's basically how I felt. Like Superman. Now my confidence was not in me. I knew where my power and peace came from. I knew it was not I that would leap over tall buildings of my own strength, but I knew that it was Him that would tear that building down to make a way where there was no way.

Chapter Thirty

What if?

After Tiffany saw that my surrender was not in her future, she once again began plotting her evil schemes. "This next one would surely work", she must have thought. "This time I will certainly destroy him", she thought. This was probably her evil reasoning. But, with God on my side I had no fear!

The next tactic was a good one. Or it was at least the best Tiffany could do at this point. She wasn't able to force me into surrender with false accusations or threats. She had to try to secure her win in another way. Tiffany had her attorney file a motion with the court requesting that the court order a social investigation. That's where the court orders someone, usually a psychologist, or a DCFS investigator to come out to the homes of each parent and interview and assess the situation.

They present their opinion to the court in the form of a lengthy and detailed report as to what they believe, in their professional unbiased opinion, would be the best parenting arrangement for the child. Judges don't have the opportunity to go to your home and visit, and they don't know anything about you, so they sometimes rely on what is supposed to be a neutral third party to assist them.

Tiffany's motion was a desperate attempt to have a corrupt counselor get involved and have them lie to the court. It was either that or she was going to once again try to coerce our son to lie to the counselor, alleging that I did something bad to him, or simply bully Jonathan into telling the counselor that he wanted to live with her full time. It was a challenge to try to maneuver my way through the gauntlet of craziness and corruption. How did I know what her plans were?

First, I believe that history is the best indicator of the future. Second, she requested the corrupt counselor she used in the past, Tina Brown. Her intent was evident.

The court scheduled a hearing date. When we arrived at the courthouse, we took a seat in the very back of the courtroom. While we were waiting our turn, Mr. Anderson and I began discussing the possible outcome of the hearing. He described that one possible outcome was that the court would deny Tiffany's request. He also described the possibility of the court granting her request, considering the judges typically see this third-party in-home analysis as a benefit for them.

It assists judges in making their decisions. If the judge granted the request, then the question would be, who would he or she appoint? The corrupt counselor of the past? A DCFS investigator? No offense to any DCFS investigators reading this, but some of them haven't had the greatest track record for honesty or integrity.

The real problem is that no matter who you bring into the situation, everyone has their own baggage to bring along with them. DCFS investigators, counselors, judges, etc. all have their own pre-determined opinions about what gender parent a child should be with, and their own bad experiences from their past that could influence their ability to make an unbiased decision. A lot of people become DCFS investigators because they were abused as children, and they grow up wanting to help other kids that are in a similar position that they were once in as a child. Because they were abused, they have a difficult time separating the person that abused them from the gender that the abuser came from, or the race that the abuser was. They tend to be so traumatized by the "man" that abused them, that they end up hating all men. Or they are so hurt by the mom that abandoned them, that they hate all women.

It's so difficult to get a fair result in cases of divorce and custody because the people making the decisions carry their own hurt, pain, and prejudices into the decision-making process. My attorney suggested we should try to come to an agreement with the opposing party, so we all have some control over the outcome. Mr. Anderson and her attorney left the courtroom and went out into the hallway to discuss a possible agreement. When my attorney came back in, he described to me what would be an agreeable arrangement concerning the motion for a social investigation. He told me that rather than allowing the judge to select whoever they want, we could each submit a list of three candidates to the court for the court to randomly select one from the total of six.

I insisted that Tina Brown would not be allowed on the list, and the opposing party agreed. The next component of the agreement would have to be that my son would not be allowed to be involved in the social investigation, meaning the counselor selected by the court would not be allowed to interview our son at all. This was a demand that I made to try to keep her from coercing him again. I figured, if she didn't agree to this, then I have absolutely nothing to lose if we simply allowed the judge to decide on the matter.

We planned to argue to the judge that it was not in our son's best interest to be placed in the middle of the battle and that it would be traumatizing to him if he were dragged into it. This was indeed a logical opinion that my attorney and I were most confident the judge would agree with us on. Then there was the matter of money. Who would pay the thousands of dollars that it would cost? I wasn't requesting it, so I didn't feel as though I should be forced to pay for something that I didn't ask for. My attorney agreed that the judge would have most likely either order her to pay for it, or worst-case scenario, make us split it. Now what was interesting is that Tiffany filed an application with the court for assistance in the cost of the social investigation, claiming that she couldn't afford to pay any part of it.

This claim was made just months after putting approximately $100,000 cash down on a brand-new house, and spending around $20,000 cash for new furniture and electronics, and $70,000 cash for college. I can't imagine how in the world Tiffany would have explained all of that, had we decided to stand in front of the judge to argue each other's side of the situation. She knew that to reach an agreement with me, she would have to agree to be responsible for the cost, and exclude our son from the social investigation, as well as the corrupt counselor. We made a deal, presented it to the judge for approval, and off we went.

Later that week, my son came home and told me that his mom said that she couldn't believe that I had agreed to this, and that I had walked right into her trap. With my son being excluded from the social investigation, her only objective now was to hope that the judge picked one of her candidates so that they could be manipulated by her and give a malicious, slanderous report that would disqualify me from having custody of my son. Tiffany was still gambling though. What if the court didn't pick one of her candidates?

What if the court actually picked an honest individual to conduct the social investigation? She would've been screwed. I suppose she had no other choice, as I had not surrendered to the threat of false allegations. If she didn't get a corrupt counselor to do this, what would be her next plan of attack? Probably moving forward with the child molestation allegations. Or maybe she would try to have me killed again. Who could know what she was going to do?

The next six to eight weeks would be spent trying to find counselors that would be willing to participate in this type of a case. I would make never-ending calls to counselors in several counties, just to find that most of them didn't want to get involved in court related work. After searching for weeks, I finally found three counselors that agreed to participate in the case, if the court had chosen them to do so. Now as for her three picks, she had no trouble at all finding the most unethical candidates to present to the court for her three options.

I researched all three of her candidates. I first went online to the Florida Department of Health's website to verify that they were licensed to practice in the state of Florida. After that, I checked to see if any of them had any disciplinary actions taken against them by the state. It was no surprise that one of them, a retired minister, had been disciplined by the state of Florida after it was determined that he acted unethically in a child custody case with the court. He was fined and penalized thousands of dollars, but he could keep his license.

How was Tiffany able to find these types of people? The ones that can be bought, and the ones that are just crazy enough to lie cheat and steal for her. I wouldn't have the first clue of how to specifically seek out and find people like this. I believe it is because she was completely sold out to witchcraft, psychic phenomena, communication with the dead, she did it all. It is my belief that when someone is not a Christian, they are not protected from witches and the curses they put on people. I have no doubt that Tiffany had sent many horrific curses my way.

They didn't have power over me because God and I have a covenant. God kept me from all evil because I am His child. I needed His reassurance and peace-keeping power at that time!

The second one she had presented, Sheila Jones, had a bad reputation. Based upon online reviews, she was dishonest and unethical as well. Unfortunately for me, she was never caught in the act by the state of Florida, like the other guy. Without hard evidence, there was nothing we could do to argue against her as a candidate. I can't remember the third candidate.

Several weeks passed, and we finally got a conference call with the judge to have her make her selection. My attorney advised her that two of my candidates had already backed out and no longer wanted to be considered, and that one of Tiffany's candidates had withdrawn as well. This left us with three candidates. Mr. Anderson presented the documentation of disciplinary action to the judge on Tiffany's second candidate and the judge agreed to exclude that candidate. So that left us with two options. The first one was a counselor that I had interviewed for the position, Matthew Perkins. He seemed to be honest and legitimate. The second one was the one that Tiffany had selected with horrible online reviews, Sheila Jones. I don't suppose that you could guess which one the judge chose, can you? Of course, it was Sheila Jones.

This would then propel me into another stage of difficulty, where I would have to figure out a way to protect myself from a potentially unethical counselor doing a social investigation to determine where my son will live for the next five plus years of his young life. This would prove to be no easy task. My attorney and I discussed possible strategies, and the best thing that I could think of would be very expensive, but I would have no choice.

To prevent the counselor from falsely alleging that I said things that I never said, I would have to hire a stenographer to be present at every meeting. Obviously, I would rather audio record the meeting, but that requires consent from all parties, and a dishonest counselor would never agree to that. A stenographer would be the next best thing. My attorney couldn't find any law that would allow the counselor to prohibit a stenographer from being present. I would now have to try to find one that would make house calls. Most of them don't, citing safety reasons, which is understandable.

After contacting about a dozen stenographers, I finally found one that agreed to come out to the house when needed. Mr. Anderson wasn't thrilled about this idea. First, he didn't believe that it was necessary. He found it hard to believe that a licensed counselor would be unethical enough to lie and cheat. I told him about Tina Brown. He also viewed the disciplinary documents on the other counselor that Tiffany had selected. Mr. Anderson was concerned that hiring a stenographer would aggravate the counselor, basically telling her that I didn't trust her.

It was a valid point. That is the message that it would have sent. However, the only other option was to allow the counselor to potentially screw me over, like she allegedly had done to other people, according to online reviews. As always, I had found myself in a bad spot. Although my attorney and I had a difference of opinion on this matter, I made my decision as to what would be done. I was prepared to move forward with the social investigation with a stenographer present to protect myself. I can only imagine how angry Tiffany would have been if I used a stenographer for the social investigation.

This plan to protect myself would have made Tiffany's plans null and void. All the money that she would spend on the counselor would have been in vain. With every word spoken between the counselor and myself being recorded in writing, there would be no way that the counselor could do anything but tell the truth. The Good Shepherd was guiding me in every decision I had to make.

Romans 8:31 states, *"If God is for us, who can stand against us?"*

I knew God was on my side because I committed my life to Him. I was praying fervently and listening for His answers. Whatever I felt prompted to do, I did.

James 5:16 states, *"The effectual, fervent prayer of a righteous man, avails much."*

I was not righteous by any holiness of my own. I was righteous because I had surrendered my life to Jesus. When I did, I received all the benefits that come when a person is born again. That is why I was so confident that God was answering my prayers in a mighty way. What a God! What a Savior!

On the other hand, Tiffany was running out of options. This was all she had left. The months were passing since the litigation started. Jonathan was getting older each day, and a little bit stronger. I know he remembered God's promise to both of us. Just like me, I'm sure he couldn't see how it could possibly happen.

After the court had selected Sheila Jones, they sent her a copy of the order requiring her to conduct the social investigation. I'm sure Tiffany thought she had won. But shortly after receiving the order from the court, for some reason, Sheila chose not to do the social investigation.

In her letter to the judge, she stated that doing a social investigation without the involvement of the child would make it too difficult for her to do the investigation properly, and therefore, she wouldn't be able to do it. She stated that she would need the child's participation to do it. Now I don't know if this was a ploy to try to change the court ordered agreement to have my son involved for coercion, but it wasn't going to work.

The court order was very specific about the terms of the agreement. No child involvement, as it wouldn't be in the child's best interest, period. What the counselor wanted or didn't want had no relevance to the court at this time. I'm not sure if this was a choice solely on the part of Sheila Jones, or if this was what she was instructed to do by Tiffany. I'm guessing it was Sheila's decision to refuse to participate.

The next step was Tiffany's attorney filing a motion to completely change the existing court ordered social investigation. In this motion, Tiffany requested that I now pay for it all, that the court orders the child's participation. Tiffany also requested that the court would allow Tina Brown to conduct the social investigation.

The court had made its decision, and it didn't work out for her, so she tried to compel the court to change its previous order. Now this was going to be interesting. If we go to court and have another hearing on this motion to change the existing court order, either one of two things could have happened. Either the court would leave the order as is, or the court would choose to change the order as requested by Tiffany, therefore admitting in fact that its previous order was inadequate. Basically, the court would have to admit that it was wrong. That was unlikely to ever happen. In order to change its previous order and allow the child's participation, it would have to ignore the fact that its previous order had acknowledged that it was in the child's best interest not to participate. Ignoring this and allowing the child's participation at this point would have required the court to willfully do what's NOT in the best interest of the child. Now while the court generally does this every day, it was doubtful that it would do it where it is documentable in writing. But then again, who knows, I was once found to be in contempt of court for paying my child support on time, and in advance. You never really know which way it's going to go. The court doesn't always use logic as its guide. And it uses the law even less frequently. It would have been an uphill battle for her to have any of it changed. Tiffany was now requesting that I pay for it after she had agreed to do so. This request was completely unjustifiable. There was no basis for such a request to even be made. Had we argued against this request before the judge, we simply would've presented the fact that the court already made its decision and that she had no basis for such a change. Certainly, having spent hundreds of thousands of dollars in cash within the past 12 months could not have indicated that she had such a dire need for financial assistance in covering the cost of the counseling, as her financial affidavit and application for indigency had indicated, as signed under oath, and under the penalty of perjury. The last thing she was requesting, was that the court order her favorite corrupt counselor Tina Brown to conduct the social investigation. Again, the court had already ruled that there would be a total of six candidates submitted to the court for consideration, and that one of those six would be selected. Three of them had withdrawn, one was ruled out do to past unethical conduct, and the one chosen refused to do it. So that left only one candidate. That was a candidate that I had selected, Matthew Perkins.

I wasn't taking any chances. I researched Matthew Perkins and found absolutely nothing negative about him. Not even so much as a bad review online. He was squeaky clean. And after I met with him, I could tell that he was an honest man. He advertised himself as a Christian counselor. That was one of the reasons that I had even considered him. I remember my son telling me that his mother was talking about how she didn't want the counselor chosen by the court to be one of those crazy Christians.

When I met with Mr. Perkins to present to him the situation and tell him what the court would require of him by, I told him about the false allegations that Tiffany accused me of. The worst accusation was of inappropriate touching. I expressed my concerns over how this could end up if she succeeded in her attempt to falsely accuse me. He sat there, very calm, which I certainly wasn't, and he asked me, "Has God spoken to you about this?". I fearfully said yes, knowing that my admission of this could come up in court and be used against me somehow, but I couldn't help it.

The power of God compelled me to be honest and tell the truth, no matter what it could cost me. I knew if I was to expect God to walk with me through this, that I would have to play by His rules. I knew that dishonesty, cheating, or any other form of action that would be in direct conflict to the character of God would basically be me taking control of the situation out of His hands, and placing it in the hands of the one who was trying to destroy me, giving him the power to succeed. I had to let my soul rest in His strength, no matter what the circumstances looked like. My walk through this fiery furnace took me down the long and narrow path that His Word promises will lead us to victory.

After answering his inquiry, he then said, "What did He tell you?" With tears running down my face, I told him what God had promised. I said, "He told me He was going to bring my baby home." Then he said with assuring confidence, "Well then, what are you worried about? You have done nothing wrong." I sat there for a moment, silent, with all the evil "What ifs" running through my mind. Satan loves to fill your mind with "What ifs". What if your health doesn't get better? What if you lose your job and can't pay your bills?

What if the airplane that you're flying in crashes? What if, what if? I had a hard time embracing the confidence that Mr. Perkins had in God's promise. It was difficult wrapping my mind around the possibility of everything working out in my favor. It never had before. I simply couldn't see a way. I now realize that the tactics of the devil can be taken by us and used against him.

Take the "What ifs" and use them for your own good. Use them to build your faith. Rather than all the negative "What ifs" that you hear, start proclaiming the positive "what ifs". Like, what if God heals me? What if I get a promotion at work? What if everything does work out in my favor? What if.......... Consider the endless possibilities, if we can just focus on the positive "What ifs?" The devil told me, "What if the judge believes her lies? Then you would lose your son, and possibly your freedom. What if?....."

I always interpreted this promise of God bringing my son home as maybe changing our parenting schedule from her having four days a week and me having three, to me being the primary custodial parent with my son living with me four days a week and living with her three days a week. I remember telling people that at a minimum, this would end with me having 51% of my son's time and her having 49%. Never did I imagine that God would do exceedingly and abundantly more than I could ever have hoped for!

I never thought, "What if" my son ends up living with me full time, seven days a week, 365 days a year. Never did I think,

"What if" this ends in the termination of her parental rights, and we move on to live happily ever after. I never thought of the "What if" God brings my baby home, and allows my new wife that He blessed me with to adopt my son, giving him the positive female role model that he had always lacked. Never did I think of these "What if's".

When I started doing this, it took the fear away, and all of a sudden, I became fully persuaded that God would do exactly what He promised. It was a real faith builder!

My mind could not comprehend the impossible becoming possible. Even though I had experienced the impossible before, I still couldn't quite imagine the possibilities that were available to me with an all-powerful, all loving God on my side. Even to this day, I have experienced miracle after miracle in my life, but sometimes I still have a hard time seeing a way through life's impossibilities. That is why I must constantly remind myself of all the impossible things God has already caused to come to pass.

I'm a tax advisor, and my mind works with facts and figures. There are no gray areas with me. It's either black, or white. It's either yes or no. There is no in between. It's like my mind works in a binary fashion. There are only two choices, zero, or one, right or wrong. There must be a logical explanation to everything. Not just logical, but also a documentable explanation for everything that happens, and it must be provable.

There must be evidence, otherwise it isn't real. I know that so many of us have this type of intellectual design, where everything must make sense to us. We must have tangible evidence of what it is that we are asked to believe. I understand that everyone doesn't experience God in the same way I do. With me having a mind that is so analytical and evidence based, I can't help but to think that if I can believe in the impossible, there is a possibility that others can believe too.

The only thing I can tell you are the things I have seen and heard, and what I've experienced. Miracles do happen, and they happened to me and my family. Ask yourself, what would I gain from telling you something that isn't true? How would I gain by telling you how I have witnessed God's work in my life? You might think it's because I want to sell books, or that I want my story told. I can tell you that none of those things are true. First, I will promise that any profit made from this book will not be kept by me. It's not about the money, it's about God. I will give away all profits made from this book to charitable organizations. If you have purchased this book and are reading it, you have just contributed to a charitable organization and have played a part in making the world a better place.

I have never been the kind of person that has enjoyed attention. I personally find all attention that is directed towards me to be very uncomfortable. Attention is the last thing that I desire, so much so that I will not use my real name when publishing this book. My story isn't what I'm telling. I'm telling you His story.

He is the author and finisher of my faith. (Hebrews 12:2). I am simply a city on a hill, that cannot be hidden. (Matthew 5:14). Jesus once said, "If they remain silent, the rocks will cry out" (Luke 19:40) I simply cannot remain silent. After all that He has done for me, I can't contain the joy. I can't keep it inside. It's like a secret that has to be told. When you have experienced as many miracles as I have, you become fully persuaded. I will tell of His greatness until my last breath is taken!

I know that sometimes, some of the greatest things in this life simply don't make sense. And some of the worst things in life also don't make sense. Like why our loved ones die too soon. Why children must suffer a lifetime of abuse? There are a lot of things that are beyond our control, and when we see God work in our lives to make the impossible become possible, we begin to build this trust in Him, knowing that as His Word has promised in Romans 8:28 that, "All things will work together for the good of those that love Him".

I look and see the impossible, and somehow, I tend to accept that it is what it is, impossible. There is no way that my health can improve. There's no way that the money that I made this year will be enough. There is no way that I can win. After all, every attorney I have ever met told me so. Somehow, while my eyes can't see the way, God always makes a way. Just one year ago medical tests such as an echo cardiogram, a stress test, and a heart catheterization all told me that my heart was severely dysfunctional. I couldn't walk from my couch to my refrigerator without losing my breath.

For a year, there was no hope. There was no way. I was basically planning my own funeral. And now, one year later, my annual follow-up tests tell me that my heart is functioning perfectly. It is working better than it was before it stopped working right. The cardiologist couldn't explain it. I couldn't even accept it. I thought for sure one of the reports had been wrong. Either the report that said that my heart wasn't working correctly was wrong, and it was never bad, or, this new report was wrong, and my heart is still dysfunctional. It couldn't be a miracle. There wasn't a logical, provable explanation for this. All I had were two medical reports, approximately twelve months apart, that stated two completely opposite results. There was no medicine taken, no surgeries performed that could have bridged the gap from severely dysfunctional, all the way to perfectly functional. I had no explanation. What allegedly had happened couldn't happen. It was impossible.

Then, there was diabetes. I had diabetes for several years. It wasn't too bad, it was under control, but it was still diabetes none the less. My A1C blood sugar levels had been as high as 7.4. In the spring of 2017 my doctor gave me diabetic medication. I never used it. I have always hated medicine. Several months passed, and it was time for my semiannual blood work. Without the medicine I was certain that it would've gotten worse. After all, it had been getting worse each year. Why would I expect anything different?

In the late summer of 2017, I went back to my endocrinologist to get the results of my most recent blood work, and when he told me what they were, my jaw literally dropped. For the first time in many years, my A1C blood glucose level had dropped below a 6.0, down to a 5.9. I couldn't believe it. I had done nothing to accomplish this on my own.

I continued to defy my doctor's recommendation for medicine. After years and years of elevating blood glucose levels, it had suddenly dropped to its lowest level in more than 5 years. I had watched my A1C slowly creep up each year, little by little it climbed. Then, in an instant, it dropped down to a normal level. There are no words that I can use that would ever be able to express my emotions over this miraculous blessing that God has given me.

Chapter Thirty-One

Pride Goes Before Destruction

As time passed, I believed Tiffany was beginning to see that there was no way out. The motion to change the social investigation was the only legal option that remained. With things going more and more in my favor as time went on, the concerns would become stronger that with nothing more she could do legally, she would begin to move toward the non-legal approach she had utilized so much in the past. My family and I had once again begun to wonder what else Tiffany would try. When she gets desperate, she gets violent and irrational.

It was also much harder to send Jonathan back to her several times a week. He was miserable and scared to death of her. My son was struggling to function in the chaos and insanity. Jonathan was completely aware of everything that was going on. Tiffany would talk about it all in front of him and she would actually discuss it with him. I had no choice but to inform him of what was happening to a certain measure. Kids should not have to be pulled apart by the legal system.

I was forced to tell him about the false allegations she made in the petition. I also had to tell him about the counseling to prepare him in case he had to be interviewed by the counselor, so he could be aware of how important it would be to tell the truth, and what the consequences of giving into the fear of his mother could bring. I can't even begin to imagine what he was going through on the inside. I will always be proud of him for having found the strength to stand against his greatest fears.

Knowing there was no way any court in the world could possibly give in to her request for changing the social investigation order was not enough for me to be able to sleep at night. I knew I couldn't leave my future and the future of my son in the hands of the court.

With the new motion to change the social investigation on my attorney's desk, we decided it was time to unleash the wrath of God onto her, and schedule a time to take her deposition. I figured if the court did grant her request to change the social investigation order, not only would I need a stenographer present at every meeting of the investigation, but I would need to bring with me some evidence of her character and mental status.

I knew we would be able to document numerous counts of perjury during the deposition, which would at least prove to a counselor the fact that she was dishonest, and that anything she said couldn't be believed.

I also knew the deposition would paint a clear picture of her mental health, and that the deposition would be like a sword in my hand.

Choosing the perfect time to do the deposition was difficult, because the moment you do the deposition, you are basically revealing your entire battle plan to the opposing party. They know your entire strategy. They will know every argument you are going to make in court, giving them plenty of time to formulate a defense which would be based mostly on lies. Were we ready to take it all to the next level? It wasn't an easy decision, but I decided that it was time to take my defense up to the next level.

After finishing the deposition, I remember telling my girlfriend, Erica, now my wife, that it was a bloodbath. Her deposition went on for 3.5 hours, but we had to stop because the court reporter had another appointment to go to. When we ended the deposition, it happened rather abruptly. The court reporter had not indicated previously that there was a time limit. I suppose she never thought it would last that long. When she told us we had to stop, I remember looking into my briefcase with a mountain of documents and another hundred questions to go through, and I told my attorney, "We have barely scratched the surface. We are only about 35-40% complete." He told me we would have to schedule another deposition at a later date. I told Erica that if we had continued all the way to the end and finished the deposition, that rather than just being a bloodbath, we would've had to call a coroner. I mean, there was almost literally blood splattered all over the walls (Metaphorically speaking of course). Had we gone another hour or two she would not have had a pulse.

I honestly don't know where to begin with describing the deposition. We did the deposition in July 2016. I literally spent a couple of months after tax season preparing for this battle. I gathered all the documents that I needed in order to formulate the questions that would need to be asked. I ended up with two small suitcases full of documents. I'm talking about all the legal documents that were filed with all the allegations, and at least a hundred emails of communication between the two of us that documented either her harassing me, her lies or simply her mental health condition.

In addition, I had organized and highlighted all the significant information on the financial documents that she actually did provide. There was a stack of other documents. Documents that would assist me in proving that she was lying about her finances. I had documents that would prove that she was involved in occult practices. I had documents proving that this most recent round of litigation was fueled by her hate towards God, and her hate towards the faith that Jonathan and I have.

The documents I had in my possession would illustrate her unjustified and unprovoked hate towards me, and clearly illustrate the dark, evil life that Tiffany and her husband lived. While I'm not judging, I'm simply saying that her choices were not the kind of choices that could contribute positively to the well-being of a young man. Tiffany's life of chronic and severe mental illness, mixed with her participation in witchcraft, and sexual immorality and debauchery were being lived out right in front Jonathan.

While I understand that no one is perfect, I also understand that what you expose your children to when they are young will shape their thoughts, their values, and their character for years and years to come. The Bible states for a parent to train up their children in the way they should go, and when they are old, he will not depart from it. Proverbs 22:6. God honors right choices.

Tiffany was telling the court she was the best parent for our child, and that my presence in his life was detrimental to him. If she had the nerve to make such a ridiculous and false statement in a court of law, under oath, where our lives were at stake, I felt as though I had the right to challenge her to prove it. Proving those statements was impossible for her. There was no way that Tiffany could support those lies. She got herself into this. Now it was up to me to show her the way out. It was time to put up or shut up. The days of lies, false allegations and threats were ending. The days of my son and I living in fear, living under the threat of violence and abuse were finally coming to an end.

Ecclesiastes 3:1, *"To everything there is a season and a time for every purpose under heaven."*

The documents were printouts of her Facebook pages, her twitter pages, and her blogs. Tiffany was addicted to using the internet as her online journal. She would use the internet to talk about truths that she could not talk about anywhere else. She thought no one would know.

Luke 12:2, *"There is nothing covered that shall not be revealed; neither hidden that shall not be known."*

Tiffany thought that the One who promised to save my son wouldn't know the truth. She thought that she could hide all the evil she had done and that it would remain hidden. I would have to presume that Tiffany has never read God's Word. If she had, and if she had believed in God's Word, I suppose I wouldn't be writing this book. In the years preceding this final round of litigation, I knew it was coming, as God had promised. I had spent years preparing for it. I was building an arsenal that would rival that of the world's greatest superpower.

God wouldn't promise you the impossible without making a way for it to become possible. He wouldn't send me into the lion's den, without His grace to protect me. He wouldn't send me to face the giant, without giving me a sling and a stone. He began equipping me several years earlier, with tools and information that would assist me in the legal battle to bring my son home. He wouldn't let me walk into this empty handed.

As I was preparing for the deposition, I knew that with Tiffany being a pathological liar, she wouldn't be able to resist the urge to lie each chance she got. All I had to do, was ask Tiffany a question pertaining to something that I could prove with a printout of her online publishings, and the majority of time she would lie about it. It wasn't my intent to make her look bad, she did that just fine all on her own.

I had to prove that she was a pathological liar to discredit her and defend myself against the false accusations that she was making against me. My intent was that the documents I had would simply be used for my defense. If I intended to use any of the information I had on her to gain any offensive advantage, Tiffany would be reading this book from behind bars, just for the crimes that I can prove, such as child abuse, federal tax evasion, welfare fraud, perjury, and many others. That's not even counting the crimes that I can't prove, such as attempted murder, stalking, vandalism, etc. Those crimes, if I could prove them, would most likely add up to life in prison. If I had any malicious or self-serving intentions, her and her husband would be wearing bright orange jumpsuit's right now. The tools that I was equipped with were intended not for obtaining justice, not for the purpose of obtaining revenge, but only for the purpose of fulfilling God's promise of bringing my son home. I am aware of God's Word about revenge, forgiveness and mercy. (Deuteronomy 32:35, Matthew 6:14, Matthew 5:7)

In the summer of 2016, while I was preparing for this deposition, my girlfriend Erica and I had been talking about the case. While I was going through and re-reading all the documents, highlighting things of interest, and formulating my battle plan, the subject of God's promise had come up in conversation. I had told her about this two years earlier. I'm not sure if she believed it.

As ridiculous as I'm sure it sounded to her, Erica didn't let it scare her away. Being raised in Christianity herself, I'm sure Erica thought it was simply faith, or positive thinking. I'm sure she never thought it to be more than that. I had shared with her other times that I heard a word from God, and all the evidence that I had to support the claims.

I learned that documenting the experiences either in writing, such as a post on Facebook, or an email to myself, both of which have a date and time attached to it, or by telling others of what I had heard, such as my mom, dad, and siblings, then when God's word would come to pass, they'd remember what I told them. With it documented before it happened, it would be my proof, or evidence that I required in order to even believe it myself.

As we were talking about this, Erica asked me, "How sure are you that you are going to win?" Without hesitation, my soul cried out, "One hundred percent." This makes me think of the old saying, that there are only two things in life that are guaranteed, death and taxes. While I would agree that death and taxes are both guarantees in this life, I must humbly disagree with the statement of them being the only two things.

You see, in addition to death and taxes, the one other thing in this life that is also guaranteed is that every one of God's promises will be fulfilled. As experience has proven to me, this is guaranteed. Every promise that you read in His word, every promise that His Son has made will be fulfilled. He will come again. He will reign over all the earth. His Father's will shall be done, on this earth, as it is in heaven. The promise that death has no control over us, is true. It is all true. We can all go through this life, all the trials, all the pain and difficulties, and know the moment will come where we will stand in His presence. We will see our name written in the Lamb's book of life. We will see His glory, and we will stand with Him, face to face. There will be no more pain, no more tears. There is the promise of everlasting life, of everlasting peace, and of everlasting joy. Everything that is good, and lovely and pure will never end. I will someday spend my eternity doing what I love doing more than anything else, praising and worshiping Him. Not from a distance, but while standing in His glorious presence. These promises, I can be sure of.

After spending several months preparing for the deposition, it was finally about to begin. It was scheduled to begin at 9:00 AM at the office of the court reporter. I would always bring someone with me as a witness, just in case she would once again make false accusations against me. My mother came with me and took a seat in the waiting room while my attorney and I walked into the meeting room. The court reporter was the next to come in and take a seat. She began setting up her equipment, and then Tiffany and her attorney walked in and took their seats.

I don't remember the name of her attorney, but she was a very young lady, about twenty-eight years old. She received her law degree three years earlier and was working for one of those ambulance chasing law firms. After twenty years of business management experience and interviewing, hiring, training and managing more than three hundred and fifty employees throughout the years, I had developed an ability to read a person and determine their strengths, weaknesses, and be able to assess if they had a future in their chosen profession.

I give the girl credit for going to law school and passing the Florida Bar, but I must admit that I was blessed by the fact that Tiffany had chosen the attorney that she did. She was not aggressive at all. She was very soft spoken, shy, and timid. My attorney was like a kitten behind closed doors. You would think that he was going to be passive and easy going. While that was true in his office, when he stepped in to the courtroom or sat down at the table for a deposition, he would transform from being a kitten, and turn into one of the fiercest lions that you would ever see.

Tiffany's attorney was not experienced enough to handle this kind of case. I could be the best tax advisor in the world, but if you bring me inaccurate information, or withhold information, the tax return is not going to be accurate. It's not always the fault of the professional. Sometimes the client is a train wreck.

I had prepared hundreds of questions for Mr. Anderson to use, like a script, every word was written out beforehand. I had separated all the questions into categories and attached all the supporting documents to each list of questions. I handed Mr. Anderson the first folder, with basic questions, such as, what is your name, what is your address, where do you work, how long have you lived at your current address, etc. We spent around thirty minutes just gathering background information. We then began to address each one of her allegations in her petition to modify custody. Now this was the fun part because it was my vindication. I had documentation to prove that Tiffany was guilty of every ridiculous allegation that she made under oath against me.

Tiffany had stated under oath in the court filing that one of the behaviors or acts that I had engaged in that was causing Jonathan severe psychological trauma, was that I was allegedly referring to our son by names other than his legal name, such as childish baby names, that would embarrass him and traumatize him. Now the truth was that she was the one that would do this. From the time our relationship ended, she refused to refer to him by his name, John or Jonathan, because that is my name too. She simply couldn't stand hearing my name spoken in her presence, so she banned the name of John from ever being spoken again in her presence.

She renamed him Bubba. She had her entire family refer to him as Bubba. She even put the name Bubba on his school enrollment forms at his middle school in 2014 when she enrolled him. Not only that, but when she got married in 2005, she started using her husband's last name as his last name and would call him Bubba O'Connor. So, while questioning her about this allegation, I handed my attorney a t-shirt she had made with the name Bubba O'Connor on it. It was a shirt she made for him for a race that she had Jonathan participate in. It had his race number on the front, with the name Bubba O'Connor on the back. After presenting this to her and asking additional questions pertaining to this topic, it was made clear that not only was she lying about me, but she was actually doing it herself.

I have mentioned earlier in this book, that a person with Borderline Personality Disorder does what the profession of psychology calls projection. It's a behavioral pattern where they will accuse you of doing what they themselves are guilty of doing, projecting their actions and behaviors onto the opposing party.

This is very concerning considering the fact that she was accusing me of touching and rubbing our son in private and inappropriate places, as she described in the court documents.

I had my suspicions concerning Tiffany, because of her abuse as a child. Many times, the child that is molested becomes the adult who does the molesting, unless there has been some type of counseling to bring healing to the victim. I was never able to prove that Tiffany had molested him, but the fact that she accused me of everything that she did, is evidence enough for me.

Tiffany was surprisingly quick to admit when questioned, that the meaning behind her allegation was along the lines of me allegedly patting him on the shoulder or placing my hand on his head while in public locations, such as at school or the super market. By this point, almost a year had passed since she made up the allegation. Our son was twelve and a half years old when she made the allegation, and now he was thirteen and a half. I suppose that she realized she had come to the divide in the road and finally had to choose which way to turn.

A year can change a lot in the life of a child that young. Jonathan wasn't the same scared, timid and powerless child he once was. He was still afraid of her, but Jonathan knew that God was on his side. In addition to my faith, Jonathan had his own faith now. He was confident he could walk through the fire and not be burned. Tiffany knew making up cruel and sick accusations and saying that I had molested our son would backfire on her, as our son could no longer be coerced into lying for her. She had no choice but to abandon that spiteful strategy and move on.

Without that strategy, Tiffany would have nothing left to try to convince a court that I was a monster and should have my son taken away from me. Tiffany always had the whole "Mr. Stone converses with a higher power" garbage. But that didn't work out quite so well for her either. Remember the behavior of projecting? Here it was again. Over the years of collecting her blogs and online journals, I had enough evidence to prove that she was once again accusing me of what she had been guilty of.

In her online postings, Tiffany would tell about her and her husband's friendship with a psychic medium named Seth and his wife Kathryn. She would frequently post about their involvement in the occult and their involvement in witchcraft. The one specific topic that she discussed in her online postings was that her, her husband and their psychic friends had started an online psychic website called Psychic Services Inc. On this website, they would make and post videos of various occult activities, such as psychic readings, and past life regressions.

When my attorney asked her, "Do you participate in activities such as speaking to the dead? Tiffany answered, "Not regularly". In other words, she was saying, "I've done it on occasion, but not like on a regular basis. Only occasionally." Her husband had written short stories about the occult and psychic mediums. Psychic mediums act as a channel to (supposedly) communicate with dead friends and relatives. That type of occult activity is called necromancy.

Necromancy is condemned by God because it opens up a door into the demonic realm. Tiffany's husband posted the stories on their website. He even had copyrights for his writings. The depth of their involvement in the occult was alarming to me. I did not want my son living in such an evil dwelling. The evidence of such involvement was very useful in formulating our argument for Tiffany projecting her misdeeds onto me. The pattern would only continue. Tiffany alleged in her petition that my finances had changed justifying an increase in the amount that I paid her for child support.

The truth was that it was her finances that had changed, and they had changed for the better. Till this day, I still don't know how Tiffany and her husband had acquired such wealth, considering they had only a few years earlier declared bankruptcy, and her husband was the only one working, earning approximately $50,000 a year at the county sheriff's office. My attorney asked her where she had gotten more than $100,000 cash to use as a down payment for a new house she had purchased just twelve months earlier. Her answer was that her mother-in-law had given it to her and her husband, a mother-in-law that lived in a mobile home park, in a single wide modular home. Then, Mr. Anderson asked her if it was a gift or a loan. Tiffany told him that it was a gift. Then, when asked about whether her mother-in-law filed a federal gift tax return, she realized that she had backed herself into a corner. She told Mr. Anderson that she didn't know, and that she has nothing to do with the family expenses. Tiffany said her husband handles all the household finances. Mr. Anderson wanted to clarify whether Tiffany had signed any documents pertaining to the federal taxation of this alleged gift from her mother-in-law, or any other documents indicating that it was a loan. She said no. After realizing that by lying about the money and alleging that her mother-in-law had given it to her, which we all knew wasn't true, she had just thrown her mother-in-law under the bus, so to speak, setting her up for possible federal tax evasion charges.

This was monumental! While we had already come out of the gate running, with our horse in the lead, this was quite a blow to her case. Tiffany unwittingly revealed that she was either lying about where all the money came from, or that her mother-in-law had committed federal tax evasion. It left her in a tough spot. She would have to choose whether to throw her mother-in-law under the bus, or herself. Tiffany's lies got her into a no-win situation. In addition to all the cash that she had used as a down payment for a brand-new house, Tiffany had also spent at least $20,000 cash on brand new furniture and electronics for the new house. She had foolishly posted comments about all the money she had spent at the furniture store, with very specific figures.

Tiffany bragged about all the thousands of dollars' worth of TVs and surround sound systems that she had purchased for the new house in 2015. Having the printouts of her blogs in our possession, my attorney asked her what the value was of her furniture and home appliances. She said she didn't know, exactly.

My attorney presented her with her financial affidavit filed with the court, under oath, showing that she had listed $1,000 as the total value of furniture that she owned. He asked her if that was correct. She said, "Yes". He then asked her how she furnished the new house that her and her husband had recently moved into. She told him they moved most of the furniture from their old house to the new house. Then he asked if it was possible that she could have purchased about $14,000 worth of furniture for the new house.

Tiffany said, "Well I suppose I bought a couple of things". Mr. Anderson presented her the printout of her blog where she bragged about spending $14,000 at Ashley furniture. When she saw this, she became speechless. Mr. Anderson asked her where she got the money for all of this, considering she reported that she has no income. Tiffany responded by telling my attorney that her husband handles all the finances, and she doesn't know. With each question about finances that was asked from this point forward, she would simply answer, "My husband handles all the household finances, I don't know anything about it." She saw that she was caught lying under oath several times. It was actually dozens of times.

Tiffany wouldn't admit that she was lying, even after being caught red handed. What did she do? She threw her husband under the bus, telling Mr. Anderson that she knew nothing about her finances, and that her husband knew everything. Mr. Anderson told her, "Since you know nothing about your finances, and your husband does, we will have to depose him and your mother-in-law as well." She refused to answer any other financial questions. Including, where she got $5,000 to place in her retirement account just months after filing for bankruptcy.

The financial documents that she submitted, even though she withheld many, were enough to paint the picture.

Within the first hour, she had thrown everyone but herself under the bus, including her husband and mother-in-law. In the first hour alone, we had many counts of perjury, tax evasion, and falsifying court documents. Then we moved on to welfare fraud. That's right. After the litigation began, we each had to submit financial documents to each other, which included tax returns. Her tax returns indicated income of around $50,000 a year for her and her husband. When I saw this, I couldn't help but to wonder how she had qualified for welfare.

Tiffany had applied for and received Medicaid benefits from the state of Florida for many years for our son. She even had our son get free lunch at school. During the years before this round of litigation, when she received Medicaid for our son, I didn't know what their household income was. Now that I did, I knew it didn't seem right that the State of Florida would provide free health care insurance for a child that lives in a household of three, with $50,000 of income.

I did some research online and found that the application for welfare benefit's in Florida specifically stated its requirement for the applicant to report all household income, including income from a spouse, and anyone else that lives in the household. It also indicated that her household income as stated on her tax returns was above the states income limitations to qualify for benefits. Earlier in the deposition, my attorney had inquired and confirmed from Tiffany that she and her husband had lived together continuously from the date of their marriage until the present time.

When we brought up the topic of Medicaid, she couldn't lie and allege that she applied for it at a time when she and her husband were separated. There was no way out of this one. Mr. Anderson asked her how she qualified for welfare benefits with the earnings that were reported on her tax return.

He presented to her a printout of the state's income limitations, clearly showing that her and her husband, did not qualify to receive tens of thousands of dollars in welfare benefits from the State of Florida and its taxpayers. Of course, she replied with "No comment". "When you applied for welfare, did you report your husband's income on the application?" Mr. Anderson asked. "No comment" she replied. At this point, she could see the writing on the wall.

Earlier in the deposition, before things had gotten so heated and uncomfortable, I decided to have some fun and offer Tiffany's attorney an opportunity to make a deal. During the first fifteen minutes or so, while my attorney was asking Tiffany some basic questions, I had taken my yellow legal pad and wrote in big letters, "Do you want to make a deal before it's too late?", and I held it up so that Tiffany's attorney could see it from across the table. Tiffany's attorney was taking notes during the deposition, and paused for a moment and looked up. When her attorney saw my sign, she giggled. She tried not to but couldn't help it.

I would've been willing to stop the deposition and write up a deal that would have been beneficial for both of us. I honestly don't know why I would have considered that. I would've proposed something like every other weekend for her, with our son living with me full time. I was well aware for years that it was not in the best interest of our son to ever be in her care, but I had been taught by the legal system that my gender was detrimental to my chance of obtaining custody of my son.

Considering I was at such a disadvantage, I should always be realistic and be willing to settle for as much as I could. I knew that agreeing to just every other weekend, just four days a month, would be harmful to our son, it was still better than the current circumstances, which was 16 out of every 28-day period with her. I was logical enough to know that 4 days of abuse and fear wasn't as bad as 16 days of it. I would have considered that a victory.

I had no idea that God had so much more planned for us. After the amusing note was presented to her attorney from across the table, she didn't stop the deposition to respond to my proposal. A couple of minutes later, I wrote her another note, saying, "Time is running out".

After that I wrote "Last chance". Then there was "Going, going, ...", and several minutes later, with no response from her attorney, I decided that this was getting too good for me. Time had just run out. We had already gotten into the whole speaking to dead people thing, and a little bit into the financial questions. So, my last note to her attorney after "Going, going...." was "GONE".

That was it. No more chances. My God had brought us close enough to the finish line. I finally had the end in sight. The rest of the deposition was just icing on the cake. We continued the deposition for a total of three and a half hours. We were forced to end before we were finished because the stenographer had another appointment to go to. We concluded the first half of the deposition with enough information to bury her. Tiffany could only wonder what we had left. She knew the deposition was to be continued. We had so much more to discuss!

I remember my mom walking in the meeting room after everyone else departed. I had been gathering up all my file folders, and she asked me how it went.

I simply quoted her Galatians 6:7, *"Do not be deceived, for God cannot be mocked. Whatever a man sows, that he will also reap."*

Tiffany had laughed at God, willfully challenging Him. Blatantly defying Him, following the will of the Evil One. She would bask in her own glory. The glory of having caused so much damage, and so much pain and destruction. Tiffany left a path of destruction everywhere she went, hurting everyone in her way. She hated God so much that in one of her blogs, she posted a comment about how much she hated God and mocked everyone that believes in Him. Since one of her allegations against me was about my faith in God, obviously twisted in a perverse manner, it seemed as though the topic of faith was on the table.

During the deposition, my attorney, Mr. Anderson, asked Tiffany about her faith, and if she had ever stated that she hated the God that my son and I believe in. Tiffany lied, and said she never did, and said that the legal proceeding wasn't motivated by her hatred toward my faith or Jonathan's faith. Then, Mr. Anderson presented her with the printout of her blog, where she states, "I hate God......" She had nothing more to say after having been caught again in a lie under oath.

Chapter Thirty-Two
Are We Going to Make it to The Finish Line?

The next several weeks continued to be interesting. The tide had turned, and the path to the promise was beginning to be formed. As Jonathan continued to come home from her house each week, he would tell me of how she would go into her rages, throwing things and acting crazy. Jonathan told me that after the deposition, she brought him with her to her attorney's office. He told me that while he was sitting in the waiting room, he could hear his mother screaming at her attorney at the top of her lungs.

He told me of how for weeks later, he would hear his mother yelling and screaming, and then talking to herself, saying "I'm not a criminal, I'm not a criminal! He's the criminal!" Jonathan would describe how she would constantly be talking to herself, literally having conversations with what appeared to be no one but herself. I asked him if it were possible that she was talking to her husband, Kaleb. He said no. He said that Kaleb wasn't home when she was doing this. I asked if she had a phone in her hand or a Bluetooth headset on, and he told me that she didn't.

The months of July, August, September, and early October 2016 were very difficult. Jonathan still had to live with her, and he told me all about the chaos and pandemonium. Tiffany held Jonathan responsible for all her woes. She thought Jonathan was the one that told me about how much she spent on the furniture. My son told me how his mom said to him that she doesn't want him, and that she is glad that he wants to live with me, because she would be better off without him.

Tiffany was everything a parent was not supposed to be. I recognized early on in our relationship that she didn't have the nurturing skills in her. Somehow that didn't stop me from having a child with her.

I saw how she related to her nephews, Brandon, and Brad, and how she lacked the basic skills to be a decent mother. One time when we were babysitting her nephews, I was joking around with the youngest one, Brad, who was probably only three years old at the time, and I showed him a picture of Tiffany and I in the newspaper when we were interviewed for the DJ business we had started in 2001. I knew Tiffany was insecure and had a very delicate and damaged sense of self-worth and value.

Tiffany had shown jealousy over how her nephews enjoyed having fun with me. She voiced her discontent over how she felt they preferred me over her. I honestly didn't think much of it. I was always great with kids, would always play and have fun with them, like I was one of them. They appreciated that, and could easily connect with someone that showed them positive attention.

So, I grabbed the newspaper and showed it to Brad. I pointed to the picture of Tiffany and I, and I asked him, who's your favorite person in the whole world? I did this because I thought he would say in a soft little voice, Auntie Tiffany.

I did this, thinking that after hearing that, it would boost her self-esteem, showing her that her nephews loved her. I never thought he would pick me. I had only known them for maybe seven to eight months at that time. But much to my dismay, when he opened his little mouth to answer my question about who his favorite person in the whole world was, the name that came out his mouth wasn't Aunt Tiffany, it was my name. He said "John". At that moment I began to panic.

I knew that I had just gotten myself in trouble, and that this three-year-old boy was my accomplice. An innocent question with good intentions had gone horribly wrong. It felt like a nuclear power plant had just experienced a meltdown and radiation was leaking, spilling out all over everyone within a radius of several miles. The wheels in my mind began spinning, trying to formulate a solution to this catastrophe. Fortunately for me, Tiffany decided to leave the room and walked towards the bathroom. When I saw her shut the door, I knew that was my chance to stop the radiation from leaking. I grabbed the newspaper again, and asked Brad, "Brad, can you do your Uncle John a favor?" He said "Yes". So, I said, "Can I ask you again who your favorite person in the whole world is, and when I do, can you point to the picture and say Auntie Tiffany?" He replied, "Yes".

I was relieved, even if it were only for a moment. I had come up with a solution that would stop the storm that was surely soon to come. When Tiffany opened the bathroom door, walked out and came back out to the living room, I held up the paper again and said, "Brad, who is your favorite person in the world". I thought for sure this was it. I thought that I would be able to save myself with this one word that would soon come out of the mouth of a child.

As I grinned with excitement, waiting for what was truly just a moment, but a moment that seemed like forever, he opened his little mouth and replied, "John". That was it. The nuclear power plant had just blown up. There was radiation in the atmosphere, and no one was safe. I could hear the sirens blaring, warning all living creatures to evacuate. Unfortunately for me, there was nowhere for me to run, nowhere for me to hide that would be safe. I had asked an innocent three-year-old to do a small favor for his favorite uncle, and that was to save me from certain destruction, but he wasn't able to do it. I asked him to lie. He was so young and innocent, with the heart of a child, he could do nothing but tell the truth.

While she remained calm at the moment, I could see the rage in her eyes. I knew that not even the EPA could clean up this mess. Hundreds of men in hazmat suits could come to clean up the radiation spillage, but it was too late. The damage had already been done. So needless to say, there would be an epic World War III battle upon leaving her sister's house. Anyway, the purpose for me sharing this story, is to illustrate that my observation of her lack of parenting skills earlier in our relationship obviously had been ignored by me, being another one of my many failures in this situation. If you know someone isn't going to be a good parent, you shouldn't have a child with them. That was my fault.

I could blame Tiffany for being a horrible parent, which she certainly was, but I can't avoid responsibility for all that my son had endured and suffered, because I knew she wouldn't be a good mother. But in my defense, I could never have imagined how bad she would be. Only God knows the hearts of men and women. He should have been the One whom I was seeking.

My lack of life experience at the time left me unable to use the information available to me to anticipate what was to come. I couldn't foresee the consequences of my choices. This lack of experience, and lack of wisdom is the reason that young people should always seek the advice of those that are much older than themselves and listen to that advice. There's nothing wrong with admitting that you do not know everything, even though every young person believes that they do. (Proverbs 11:14, Proverbs 12:15, Proverbs 15:22, Proverbs 19:20-21)

This lack of basic parenting skills had spilled over into all the years that she was a parent. She never got any better. Just like most diseases that don't have a known cure, her mental illness only became worse with time. My son suffered so much because of this.

Months were beginning to pass after the deposition, and the smell of victory was in the air. While it was a very stressful time, I believe that she had begun to accept that defeat was coming. The motion that Tiffany's attorney filed to modify the court's ruling on the social investigation had been sitting on my attorneys' desk for months. Her attorney had not set a court date for that motion to be presented to the court.

In August 2016, Jonathan told me his mom hired another attorney. It was Julie Walker. Tiffany had hired Julie in the past, during the 2007-2008 round of litigation. Julie had a reputation in the community for being a ferocious beast of an attorney. Most other attorneys feared her. And from my limited experience with her as she represented Tiffany in 2007-2008, I could see why. She was not afraid to set truth aside in order to win. She was not afraid to set morality aside to secure a victory. Ms. Walker did not stop to look at the innocent victims, the casualties of war, as she fought. She took great pride in being good at what she did and wasn't afraid to show it. However, I soon learned that my attorney was friends with Julie. They were indeed professionals though. They never crossed the lines that separated their friendship from their jobs. They both worked hard to best represent their clients in this case, as I'm sure they did with any other case they happened to cross paths on.

There was one time in October though, when I was in a conference call with my attorney, that he said to me, "John, I shouldn't tell you this, and if you repeat it, I will deny ever saying it, but when I was on the phone with Julie this morning, she told me, "That woman is crazy. Julie simply doesn't know what to do with her...." This was refreshing to me, because while I could explain to my attorney how mentally ill, and dangerous she was, he could never fully comprehend what it was like to deal with her on a regular basis. And how this battle could in an instant change from the legal realm into the criminal realm, where the lives of my family and I could be at stake, there was no way for me to make him believe all of this.

I'm sure all of his clients tell him how crazy their ex is, and how dangerous they are, but most of the time it's the one telling you this that is the crazy one. I can understand that there was no way for him to believe me any more than he could believe any of his other clients. With her own attorney admitting she was crazy, I now felt confident knowing that my attorney believed me.

I don't understand why she would hire another attorney. She was so close to the end of the case. I can't imagine Tiffany doing this of her own free will. My guess is that her first attorney decided not to go down with the ship and told Tiffany to find herself another lawyer. It's also possible that Tiffany recognized the lack of experience of her first attorney and fearing that she might also be facing several criminal charges, decided to hire a more experienced and skilled lawyer. Whatever the reason was, hiring one of the best attorneys in the area was not going to change what God had promised. All the money that she had wasn't enough to stop her train from derailing. All the lies and all the threats were now worthless. She could have literally held a gun to my head and I would have simply laughed, knowing that the time had come (Ecclesiastes 3:1) and there was nothing she could do to harm me anymore.

Not a lot happened legally after the hiring of Julie Walker. They didn't schedule a deposition for me, they didn't schedule a hearing for their motion to change the social investigation. Everything had pretty much come to a screeching halt. The only thing that changed for me around this time was that in late August 2016 I had been diagnosed with a severe heart condition. I had gone for an echo cardiogram once a year for many years after suffering an allergic reaction to an antibiotic many years ago. The allergic reaction caused heart palpitations and an extremely high heart rate, among other things. At the time that this occurred in 2006, I had been given an EKG, and a stress test, both of which had shown abnormalities in the heart's function.

I was ordered to have my heart checked every year to monitor its condition. Subsequently, after the first year or two after the allergic reaction to the antibiotic, my heart resumed normal functioning. That was until August 2016, when the test indicated that I had severe diastolic dysfunction. This is a condition where the part of the heart that pumps blood out and into the lungs and the rest of the body isn't functioning properly, and as a result the blood can back up into the lungs, causing shortness of breath, and tightness in the chest.

What a bad time to receive such a diagnosis. It had me thinking that I might not live much longer. There was no way to know if it would get worse, and if it did, how long would it take to decline? I was now in the middle of two of the toughest battles of my life, simultaneously fighting for my life in two different ways. I remember telling my attorney about the diagnosis and asking him what would happen to my son if I died. Of course, with my absence the only legal option would be for my son to live with his mom full time.

At the time, we had not yet arrived at a conclusion to this legal case, and the thought of dying before a conclusion was made left me scared, not for my life, but for my son's life. I told my attorney that if I were to die before we finished this case, that there would be no way that Jonathan would ever go to live with her. I asked my friend Daniel, my fiancé, and my parents to be sure to look after him if anything happened to me.

I was prepared to leave them enough financial resources to be able take my son and to do whatever was necessary to keep him safe from her. The clock was ticking, and it appeared as though I was now in a race to the finish line. It was frustrating having to live on the edge of my seat each day, wondering if this fight was ever going to come to an end. It had been going on for a little more than a year, and we were no closer to victory than when we started.

The situation didn't change until one day in early October, when my son didn't want to go back to his mother's house the next day when he was supposed to. He asked me to email her to ask if he could spend another day with me. So, I did. To my surprise she agreed. She had never been cooperative in the past. For her to agree to let him stay with me another day was shocking. As I mentioned earlier, based upon what my son had been telling me for months after the deposition, the situation at his mother's house had deteriorated significantly. The conflict escalated to levels that were never before seen. Tiffany was verbally abusing him more than ever before. At this point, I believe she was close to having a complete breakdown. It was scary. My family and I were scared for his life. You witness stories all the time on the news of mentally ill parents killing their children, driving them into lakes, and all kinds of other sick and senseless stories that happen in real life. You never think that those kinds of things could happen to you, but in this situation, with this individual, anything was possible.

Jonathan stayed with me an extra day, as his mother had agreed to let us do. And then, after that one extra day, I had to drop him back off to her. It was that day, Tuesday, October 11, 2016, that everything changed. It was the straw that broke my son's back. Till this day, I still don't know exactly what happened.

Chapter Thirty-Three
My Son's Courageous Stand

On October 12, 2016 I picked up my son from school, and I could see that something serious had happened. He was like a zombie. I could see he was very shaken. It was like he was in a trance. Just simply stone cold. This was very unusual for my son. Like a lot of kids his age, he was always talkative and very energetic, and even hyper at most times. This sudden change in behavior was very noticeable. I asked him what was wrong.

He told me that his mom was very angry about him wanting to spend an extra day with me. He told me some of the things she said to him that day, but I know he never told me everything that had happened. Tiffany was so enraged that he didn't want to be with her. She told him she hated him, and she wished she had never given birth to him.

Tiffany continued her bitter and cruel tirade against Jonathan. Words so mean and malicious were spewed upon Jonathan's tender heart. I can't imagine how damaging those words were to his little soul. Even though Tiffany was a horrific mother, and he didn't want to live with her, she was still his mother. When you're a child, your mom and dad are supposed to be the two people in this world that you can always count on to love you and be there for you.

I'm a grown man and yet I can't conceive having one of my parents tell me to my face that I am worthless, I don't matter, and that I was never wanted. She has wounded him in ways that are unimaginable. It hurts my soul to think about all he has been through. Jonathan was an innocent victim. Probably some of you are thinking God, how can you allow this?

Trust me, those thoughts crossed my mind many times. There are some things we won't know until we reach heaven. Sometimes you have to step out in faith as I did for many years, and I thank God that He honored my faith and answered my prayer that my son would come home to me. At this time in my life though, I can honestly tell you that all is well with my soul. I trust that His plans for us are to prosper us, and not to harm us, and to give us hope and a future. (Jeremiah 29:11)

My hope in Him will never be lost, no matter what the circumstances are. He will always be greater than even the most difficult circumstances in life. I know that He and He alone can change things. He can heal Jonathan's heart. Sometimes you must know Him and love Him enough to trust Him with everyone that you love. Abraham did it when he was told to sacrifice his son Isaac. He was willing, and it was that willingness to put God above all else, that caused him to receive his miracle.

After his mother's final rampage against him, Jonathan didn't want to go back. Later that evening we went to church for Bible study and the youth group worship service. I asked him earlier in the day if he wanted me to email her asking her to let him stay an extra day. He said he didn't know. He was scared, shaken and hurt all at the same time. I know he wanted me to ask her, but he was afraid to do so in case if she said no and he had to go back. He was at the crossroads in his young life, where he had to make the biggest decision of his life.

He was only 13 years old and had been placed in a position to have to make what was probably the scariest and toughest decisions of his young life. No child should be in that position. Unfortunately, my hands were tied because of the law. I had no choice but to return my son to his tormentor. If I didn't, the law would have come after me. Not that I was afraid of what the law would do to me, but I was afraid of what the law would do to my son had I interfered with his mother's custody rights. I couldn't risk giving her or the court any excuse to condemn me and take him from me. It would hurt him as well as me. Making one little mistake could have ended up sending him to live with her full time. There was simply no room for errors on my part. I was walking the tightrope.

We were in the car in the parking lot of the church, just about to go in, when I asked him again if he wanted me to ask her to let him stay the next day. He was still frozen, almost lifeless. He told me, "I don't know." So, I told Jonathan to think about it and let me know after church. We went into church, and I honestly don't have any memory of what the sermon was about that night. All I remember is walking back to the car after it was all over, and seeing that my son had appeared to be a little bit more relaxed, and less tense. We sat down in the car, and as he was staring straight forward, with an intensity that could've shattered the windshield, he boldly confessed, "I'm not going back".

I sat there in silence and shock. He said in a fearful, but yet strong voice, "Email her. Ask her if I can stay another day." I said, "OK. I'll do that. But Jonathan, I must tell you that my attorney said that if she doesn't agree, that I have to let her pick you up from school". We sat in the car for a few minutes, and I sent out the email, asking to let him stay another day. She didn't respond right away. When we got home, he had to get ready for bed because he had to get up early for school.

The whole time he kept asking me repeatedly, "Did she answer, did she answer?" He was worried. He wanted to know what his fate would be. It was just a little bit before bedtime that

I got the email from her where she once again, to my surprise, she agreed to let him stay another day. He was relieved, at least for the moment.

I had not realized that on that day, October 12, 2016, that God had brought my baby home and fulfilled His promise to me. At the time, I thought it was a one or two-time thing, where she would agree to let him stay for just those one or two extra days. I had no idea that October 12th would be the date that I had waited thirteen and a half years for. I wasn't aware of the fact that it was that date that I would soon engrave on the right side of the cross that I had bought when my son was only three months old.

After October 12, 2016, the intensity level would increase exponentially. Jonathan was scheduled to be picked up by his mother two to three times a week. He made the decision to never go back, but the hard part was to figure out how to make that happen. I had to work within the law, and my attorney told me many times that as long as Tiffany agrees to let him stay an extra day, then it was fine, but if she ever chose not to agree, I had to let him go back to her. I discussed this with Jonathan, and he wasn't about to have any of that. Jonathan was adamant that he was never going back. He said, "I will never see or speak to her ever again".

So, every time it was her day to pick him up, he would ask me to email her asking her if he can stay another day. And each and every time, he would anxiously ask, "Did she respond, did she respond?" We were on the edge of our seats at all times, wondering if this was the day that she would refuse. It was a very complicated, and very intense situation. Jonathan was not going back, and that was his final decision. And while that was the "decision" that he made, it unfortunately was legally out of our control. If Tiffany said no, it was no.

Week after week passed, and it was the same thing. We sent email after email, and all then lived with the anxiety of what the response would be. She would respond with agreement every time, but we didn't believe that it would last forever. I asked my attorney what would happen if she wanted him back, and he refused to go. He told me that my son could refuse to get into her car at school if he chose to. However, if he did, her and her husband could forcefully require him to go with them, and there was nothing that could be done about it. He even said that she could call the police and have the police compel him to go with her. I had to counsel him on what his mother's legal rights were So, it appeared as though we were at the mercy of the law, and at the mercy of her decision each time we asked. Talk about being stressed and anxious. It was a part of our everyday lives.

Chapter Thirty-Four

She Said Yes!

It was in December 2016 that I got married for the first time. Erica and I had been dating for several years when I decided to propose to her on her birthday, September 19, 2016. I knew Erica was the woman I could count on when things were bad. She stood with me through horrific times. She was my encourager and the lifter of my spirit. She didn't budge when it came to the legal battles in my life. Erica was there for me, and one of very few that told me to keep fighting. By her attitude I knew she was in it with me for the long run.

Faithfulness like that is hard to find. Proverbs 31 states, "A virtuous woman who can find?" I had found that virtuous woman and I wasn't going to let her get away from me! Erica was the first one I would reach out to when things were tough or when things were going great. She was the one I wanted to share the rest of my life with. I loved spending time with her. I knew that God sent this wonderful woman into my life. Erica is also a woman of faith and lives a life that honors God. One day it hit me hard, "I am totally in love with this woman! She loves Jonathan and will be a great step mom for my son.!"

I was also more than a little nervous, with thoughts like, what if she says no? What if she says, "I just want to be friends"? My heart was absolutely pounding when I finally got up the nerve to ask her. She happily threw her arms around me and said, "Yes"! After I surrendered my life to the Lord, everything I had waited so long for, started happening quickly. While it took a long time to get to this point in our relationship, it didn't take long for us to arrive at the wedding date!

It was less than three months from the time of the proposal to the date that we had selected for our wedding. A lot of variables were considered when selecting the date for our wedding. It had to be a weekend of course, when everyone was off from work and able to attend. Then we had to plan it around tax season. January through April is too busy and we didn't want to wait eight months to get married. So, we picked December.

My life was finally coming together, and I had to make a lot of choices with my bride to be. What joy we had planning our wedding and honeymoon! We selected a date and then we booked a Golf and Country Club near our home to host the wedding. It was a beautiful facility. I wanted to enjoy every part of the engagement, and I did. We swiftly planned each part of the wedding, with excitement and anticipation of our new life together. God helped us take care of every little detail. Although we were hurried in our decisions, it was still such a joyous time for us. It was crunch time, and God gave us the wisdom and grace to get everything done before the upcoming tax season.

I have been a tax adviser for 20 years now. January 1st through April 15th is always nonstop pandemonium for me. Running four offices located in three different cities is an around-the-clock work schedule. I would be lucky if I had time to eat three meals a day during tax season. That's how busy I was. On top of all that, I had just been diagnosed with a heart condition, and was waiting for my cardiologist to schedule a date for a heart catheterization. That procedure would require a few days of rest at a minimum, but we were a little nervous as to what the doctor would find. After all, he would be looking inside of my heart.

We didn't know if they would find a blocked artery that could require a stent, or a blockage that would require open heart surgery. I had witnessed my dad go through two open heart surgeries to fix blockages in his arteries. Open heart surgery required 4-6 weeks of recovery.

So, we selected the date of December second for the wedding, but that was a tentative date, pending the outcome of my heart catheterization that I had scheduled for November 9th. I'm telling you when it rains, it really pours. Every week, we had to deal with the anxiousness of whether there would be a confrontation regarding returning Jonathan to his mother.

We also had to deal with the pressures of not only our wedding, but my health. These were certainly trying times. Our whole world was changing. It was turning inside out, and upside down. There was no certainty. There were no guarantees. We were living each day by faith. Knowing that only God's will would be done, whatever that would be.

Despite the fact that He had promised me victory, it was difficult to see victory through the eyes of a mere mortal man. The deck appeared so stacked against me. It seemed as though if one adversity didn't take me out, then surely the other one would.

I just had to keep on reminding myself, "If God is for me who can be against me?"

I also heard a lot of evil "What ifs" in my heart. What if the doctor accidentally tears an artery while navigating the instrument through my arteries, and I bleed out on the table? What if the anesthesiologist gives me too much anesthesia and I never wake up?

After several days of this, I realized this is the devil, and all the evil "What ifs" are coming from him. Instead, I decided to think only on good, godly things.

What if the procedure ends up going well? What if the doctor finds nothing wrong and I'm free to move forward with my wedding? What if....?

I'm not going to lie to you and tell you that I was able to see a way through it all. The truth is, I couldn't see any way at all. But isn't that what faith is, stepping out onto the water, when you can't even swim?

Chapter Thirty-Five

An Uncertain Future

It was November 8th, 2016, the night before my heart procedure. I had not yet told Jonathan, he had too much to deal with already. I waited until just the night before to tell him. I thought that I had to tell him, just in case something went wrong. I know a heart catheterization is a common and generally safe procedure, but there is always that one in a million chance it could go horribly wrong. If they had found a blockage in an artery that they couldn't place a stent into, I could've ended up staying at the hospital for open heart surgery. I had to let him know.

When I told him that I was going to the hospital for a surgical procedure, he asked me "Aren't you scared?" And while it was true that I was nervous, with all kinds of worst -case scenarios racing through my mind, I knew I had to be strong, because if I didn't show Jonathan my faith in God, how could I ever hope for him to have faith? At a time where I needed him to be as strong as he could possibly be, I had to show him the power of our God, through faith that knows no limits.

I walked into my bedroom and got the gold cross that I had purchased for him thirteen years earlier. I had already showed it to Jonathan once before and explained to him what it represented. I held it up in front of him, and told him, "The same God that promised me thirteen years ago that He was going to bring you home, is the same God that I trust with my life. To answer your question, No, I'm not afraid. I don't have to be."

I put him to bed after that. Before leaving his bedside, we prayed, as we always did every night. We also prayed for God to heal his mother, and to bring her peace, and we prayed that someday she would come to know Him. We thanked Him for the success of my upcoming surgery, and ended the prayer with a strong Amen!

The next morning my fiancé and I drove to the hospital, checked in, and I put on one of those gowns that you tie up in the back, the ones that can sometimes flap open, leaving your butt cheeks hanging out. I laid in the bed, nervously awaiting my turn. There was certainly a sense of anxiety flowing through my body. It wasn't until we had been there for about thirty minutes that I suddenly felt this overwhelming sense of peace.

It came out of nowhere, and instantly I was calm, and confident. And no, it wasn't drugs that made me feel that way. They hadn't given me anything yet. It was that sense of peace that I recognized as God's presence. It was at that moment that I knew everything would be ok. I told Erica that we would indeed be getting married in a few weeks. We hadn't even sent out the invitations yet. We had been waiting to see what happened as a result of the heart cath.

At that moment, I knew the wedding would take place as planned. While I was confident about this, I honestly wasn't sure what condition I would be in by our wedding date. I wasn't sure if I would have a scar running up and down my chest where they cut me open just a few weeks earlier, or if I would simply be recovering from a stent being placed in my chest. No matter what the outcome would be, I knew that I was getting married in three and a half weeks.

It wasn't long before it was my turn to go into the operating room. When I got there, they began by sticking an IV into my arm. Then they started to give me medication to relax me and dull the pain that was soon to come. I was awake during the entire procedure. There was local anesthesia at the location that the incision would be made. The first injection of lidocaine apparently wasn't enough because when the doctor went to make the incision, I could feel it, and it hurt. I told him, and they did another injection of lidocaine.

I've never used those medications before, or the dye that they injected into me. I guess the dye helps the doctor see inside of my arteries and heart. The dye caused an uncomfortable burning sensation throughout my body that would eventually dissipate. Then the pain medicine, which was called dilaudid, when first injected, caused a sense of heaviness to flow through my body starting at my waist and moving up to my head, chest and arms. I also remember that everything started to look like it was moving, specifically the ceiling. I kept asking the nurses if the ceiling was moving or if it was just me. They said "It's just the medicine, go ahead and close your eyes".

It was over before I even knew it. Right after the procedure was finished, I felt ten years younger. I had none of the aches and pains that I usually had, and I felt great. Unfortunately, it only lasted a few hours until the medicine wore off. When I got home, I was so sore I could hardly walk for a few days. With the heart catheterization procedure they make an incision and then place a tube through an artery that they access through your inner thigh, parallel with your hip. It made walking very difficult for a few days. The doctor ended up not finding any blocked arteries. Because of this finding, there wasn't a need for stents or bypass surgery. The doctor did find that the heart tissue was stiff and not pumping properly.

In other words, it wasn't working right but there was nothing that he could do to treat the problem. At this point, I was relieved that I had at least dodged a bullet, or should I say scalpel. Without the need for surgery I would be back on my feet in a few days, and back to the same routine of emailing Jonathan's mom to ask if he can stay another day.

Chapter Thirty-Six
Going to the Chapel

Week after week passed, and the stress and pressure would remain. My fiancé did most of the wedding planning. She did a beautiful job. The wedding went off without a hitch and everyone had a wonderful time. My son was the ring bearer and stood up front next to me during the ceremony. What a miracle! Leading up to the wedding we were worried something would happen with my son's mother to prevent him from even being at the wedding much less standing by my side. How good my God has been to me.

Erica and I went to Colorado on our honeymoon. Neither one of us had ever been to Colorado before. We flew from Tampa to the airport in Denver. When we arrived in Denver, we picked up our rental car, which was a Ford Fiesta. The car was no bigger than a golf cart, and had the same amount of power as one. We laughed at how ridiculous we must have looked.

We spent the first two nights in Denver at the Renaissance hotel. It was a magnificent hotel with breathtaking views of the majestic mountains. The room was huge, with an entire wall as a window. Later that night it snowed, and we had a spectacular view of the snow-covered mountains glimmering in the bright moon light. The street lights were lit up and people walking back and forth on a soft and gentle blanket of snow that had just fallen. It was so peaceful and the perfect get away for us.

After staying in Denver for the first couple of days, we drove our little Ford Fiesta to Breckenridge Colorado. We went to downtown Breckenridge to explore, have adventures and make new memories. We were in love and I enjoyed sharing this beautiful experience with Erica. There were such quaint little gift shops and great restaurants to discover.

Unfortunately, after only about an hour I started to not feel very well. My heart was racing, and it felt like it was literally going to burst out of my chest. I was feeling dizzy, like I was going to pass out, and was having difficulty breathing. I wasn't aware of the fact that Breckenridge is almost 12,000 feet above sea level, and that when you are not accustomed to that elevation, it could cause some symptoms, such as shortness of breath and fatigue. Not only did I not realize that, but considering I had a heart condition that already caused shortness of breath and fatigue, the two variables combined could be very troublesome. We live in Florida, where the elevation is only about 10 feet above sea level. The drastic change in elevation had placed an extra burden on my heart. We walked into a realtor's office to inquire about using a restroom. Immediately upon walking in to the office one of the ladies had noticed that I was having difficulty breathing. She whipped out an oxygen and heart rate monitor, the one you put on your fingertip. Apparently, she was used to seeing tourists in this type of situation. My blood oxygen concentration was 91%, which was a little low. And my resting heart rate was around 130, which was high. She invited us to sit and rest for a while. After resting for 10 minutes, we realized that I could not continue our exploration of this beautiful winter wonderland.

Unfortunately, the rental car was stuck in the snow when we went back to it. We couldn't get it out. There were a couple of guys walking by with their girlfriends/wives, and they were probably in their early to mid -twenties. We asked them if they could help us push the car out of the snow. It was embarrassing because I was only 39 years old at the time. Anyone walking by looking at me would think that I should be capable of pushing the car out myself. But the reality was that I could barely breathe just standing still.

When we got the car out of the snow, we were able to drive it back to the hotel, where the rest of our honeymoon would be ruined by my poor health at the time. Even at the hotel I was having a hard time breathing. I called my cardiologist to explain how I was feeling, and he told me it sounded like I was suffering from pulmonary edema, a condition where, due to the dysfunction of the heart and the higher elevation, blood was backing up into my lungs causing the difficulty breathing and the heart to have to try to work harder. He recommended that I go to the hospital and he told me that they would give me diuretics through an IV to help drain the fluid from my body. The doctor also advised me to get back to a lower elevation as soon as possible. My research online indicated that while Breckenridge was almost 12,000 feet above sea level, Denver was only about 5,000 feet above sea level.

We were supposed to spend another night in Breckenridge and then head over to Aspen for a few days. We ended up having to leave Breckenridge the next morning to go back to Denver. While we were in Denver a day or two before, I did have some mild difficulty breathing, but not nearly as bad as it was while in Breckenridge. Erica was a trooper. She showed such patience and understanding. Now the funny thing is that we couldn't drive back to Denver, because the Ford Fiesta that we rented once again got stuck in the parking lot, in a half an inch of snow. That thing couldn't drive on anything other than dry pavement. We had to get it towed back to Denver and upgrade to a four-wheel-drive SUV. I never thought that a half an inch of snow would require a four-wheel-drive SUV. I could ride a bicycle through that much snow, but a Ford Fiesta couldn't drive through it.

We finished the rest of our trip in Denver, very much in love and grateful for each other. When you are in love with someone, and you have difficulties, love makes everything doable. I knew how strong the love was between us, together we would see the miraculous promises of God come into our lives. When two people love each other and agree concerning their faith and other important decisions, nothing is more powerful.

We ended our honeymoon with laughter and appreciation for each other. God let me know that I made the right decision and life was already beginning to head in the right direction.

My son was at home with my parents the week we were on our honeymoon. By this time, we had gone eight weeks with my son home with me, and we were still playing the email game where we had to ask Tiffany if he could stay another day. She continued to agree up until this point. I think she realized that it was over. However, we had no idea at the time what was going through her mind.

My attorney had heard nothing at all from her lawyer during those two months that my son had been with me. I had told him that my son refused to go back to her, and he advised me to continue to ask her if he could stay, and if she agreed we would be fine, until the next time we had to ask again. We had no idea what was going on, and what would happen next. My wife and I continued to email his mom while we were in Colorado, with the fear that if she decided she wanted our son back, we would be thousands of miles away during a potential conflict. Fortunately, Tiffany agreed to let him stay the entire week. Another thing I thanked God for, was that there was not one instance of conflict concerning Jonathan and his mom while I was away.

Chapter Thirty-Seven

The Final Battle

Several weeks later, in early January 2017, I made an appointment for Erica and I to meet with our attorney. We were getting frustrated with the lack of progress in the case. I told him that I wanted it finished. He advised that we should continue going in the direction that we are, and as long as nothing changed, don't rock the boat. He said our case was getting stronger and stronger every week that my son stayed with me and didn't see her. At this point it had been about three months since he had seen his mother.

Mr. Anderson was concerned about my son's performance at school. Due to all the trauma and stress he went through, his ability to focus in school had declined, and so did his grades. Mr. Anderson cautioned me that if his mom decided she wanted him back, she could argue that letting him stay with me for three months was done on a trial basis and that his declining performance in school was evidence that it was not working out well for my son.

My son needed counseling to help him with the post-traumatic stress that he was dealing with. His whole life had been one giant nightmare of violence, abuse, and chaos. Finally, at the young age of thirteen, he had to be strong enough to stand against the beast. He still had to endure the anxiety of knowing he could be forced to go back at any time. I knew I couldn't let him go on like this. It was no way for a child to have to live.

I did bring him to talk to a pastor a couple of times, to try to give him a safe place to let out some of the pain and anxiety. I wasn't legally able to take him to a medically licensed counselor or therapist without her consent, and she would not give her consent to do so. My hands were tied regarding getting him help to cope with the trauma.

As Erica and I sat at the table across from my attorney going back and forth over the strategic options that were available to us, he again, advised me to keep asking her to keep him an extra day, several times a week, and just go with that strategy. I told him my son needed closure. I told him at that table, "Mr. Anderson, I can tell you exactly how this is going to end. It is going to end with my son's mom having her parental rights terminated." He responded by saying, "Look John, I believe you, but it's just not going to be that easy." He was patronizing me. He didn't believe me. Not one bit. After discussing the case for another ten to fifteen minutes, I had concluded that the only way to move this case forward would be to drag out the big guns, and to schedule his mother's second deposition and her husband's and mother-in-law's depositions.

This would force her into a corner, and my attorney was afraid that doing so would cause her to lash out and attack. He continued to advise that it was best to simply lay low and not to rock the boat. We had only gotten about a third of the way through her first deposition back in July, and it was a blood bath. I knew that once we scheduled and completed the second deposition, it would be the end. We had already exposed her for many of the crimes that she was guilty of, like welfare fraud, perjury, and her mother-in-law's federal tax evasion. We had already found enough evidence in the first deposition to justify motioning the court to require a psychological evaluation of her.

Unfortunately, while we could prove all these other crimes, we couldn't prove that Tiffany had abused my son for years. Not without placing Jonathan on the stand in the court room. That wasn't an option because he was still so scared of her. My son was strong enough to refuse to go back, but he knew that if he testified in court about the things she did to him, that they might not believe him, and the court could force him to go back, in which case he would've been in far more danger after ratting her out to the judge. It simply was not an option.

However, this situation reminded me of Al Capone. The feds could never prove any of his more significant crimes, such as murder. However, they were wise enough to be able to catch him on tax evasion, and they used that as their means of imprisoning him.

I instructed my attorney to contact her lawyer to schedule the depositions. Several days later he contacted me and told me that her attorney wanted to schedule another mediation first. I remember telling him it was a waste of time, that the first mediation a year ago was just a waste of time and money. He insisted that we agree, and so we did.

It was several weeks later when we met at the courthouse for the final mediation. It was February 21, 2017, and it had now been four and a half months since my son had seen his mother. I remember that morning very well. My wife was working overnight the night before and didn't get home until about 10:00 AM that morning. The mediation was scheduled to begin at 9:00 AM, so she couldn't attend. My mom and dad went with me. My mom waited in the hallway, and my dad waited for hours in the car. My mom and I walked in the building, and as always, when you go into the courthouse you must empty your pockets and take off your shoes and belt, just like at the airport.

After we went through the metal detectors and gathered our belongings, we proceeded to the directory to figure out where the mediation room was. When we got there, Tiffany and her husband were already there. Mr. Anderson hadn't arrived yet, so we sat down on a bench in the hallway to wait. The mediation attorney came out of the meeting room and introduced herself. She asked if we were ready to begin. That's when I advised her that we were waiting for my attorney to arrive.

I knew this could be a challenging meeting. I had already decided that I would not agree to anything less than what my son wanted, and that was to never see his mother again. At this point, I was tired of playing the game. I was tired of having my hands tied by the legal system. I was tired of not being able to protect my son because the law wouldn't allow me to do so. There was simply no way I would walk out of there with anything less than what God had promised me fourteen years earlier. I knew that had I been offered a deal where we each had 50/50 timeshare with him, that it would be tempting to just settle and end the battle. But if I had done that, the chaos would continue. I suppose that I would have been willing to allow her supervised visitation once or twice a month if I had to, but that's the most I would allow.

Mr. Anderson finally arrived and we began. This time I was not stressed out at all. I walked in with a boldness and strength because I knew God was with me. He was fighting this battle. There was no way the enemy could win. Tiffany and her attorney were across the hall in another meeting room. Mr. Anderson then proceeded to open his briefcase, take out my file, which at this point was as thick as half a dozen Bibles combined. He asked me, "What it is that you're willing to propose as a settlement.?" He indicated to me that Julie Walker had told him that her client was ready to finish this today. Mr. Anderson didn't believe that. Now at this point, I had continued to pay her child support each month for the past four and a half months that

Jonathan was with me. On top of that, Tiffany had not provided me with any financial support for our son during that time. So not only did I feel as though it was fair to require that she give me my money back, but since I had to give her child support for the past fourteen years, that it was only fair that Tiffany be required to provide me with some financial contribution for the past four and a half months that he had been living with me.

I told Mr. Anderson that I would require that the child support I provided her for the past four and a half months be returned to me in full. Then I told him I would require a minimum of four hundred dollars per month in child support from her for this same period of time.

This was an extremely modest amount, considering the amount of income that the court could impute to her based on the hundreds of thousands of dollars in cash she had been spending over the past two years and the income that she was trying to hide. Based upon Tiffany's document-able cash flow, child support should've been at least fifteen hundred dollars a month. But unlike her, I cared only about my son, and not about money.

I then told him I would require reimbursement of legal fees, considering that a year and a half earlier, I abided by the existing court order when I asked her to meet with me and a mediator, as was required, and she refused.

We presented these proposals first, and to our surprise, the mediating attorney came back with her proposal to surrender her parental rights, just as long as she would also be relieved of all responsibilities, most specifically, financial responsibilities.

Tiffany had never taken any financial responsibility for our son in his entire life. I had always provided all of Jonathan's financial care either directly, by purchasing all of his clothing and other needs, and then also indirectly by providing her money that was supposed to have been used for his care. The only thing she ever bought for our son with the money I provided her was groceries to feed him the four days a week that he was with her. The amount I had been giving her every month was more than enough to provide him with food the sixteen days each month that Jonathan was with her, with excess left over.

Before Tiffany committed welfare fraud and began receiving Medicaid and free lunch for our son at school, she would send him to school every single day for years with a peanut butter and jelly sandwich, a bag of chips, and a juice pouch. She did this literally every day for years. Each time that I would pick Jonathan up from school on a day that she had brought him to school, I would empty out his lunch bag to prepare his lunch for the next day. And every day, year after year, he would come home with a lunch bag that had a squashed peanut butter and jelly sandwich, which he didn't eat, an empty sandwich bag from the chips, and an empty juice pouch.

So early on in his school years, when I saw this, I would ask him what he was eating, and he told me that he would just eat the chips and the drink. I asked him why he wasn't eating the peanut butter and jelly sandwiches, and he told me he didn't like peanut butter and jelly sandwiches. I asked him if he ever told his mom that he didn't like them, Jonathan told me that he was afraid to tell her. I couldn't let my son go several days a week with nothing more than potato chips and a juice pouch for lunch. So, I would go to his elementary school each week and give the cafeteria cashier ten to fifteen dollars each week, so he would be able to buy lunch and eat on the days that Tiffany brought him to school. On the days that I brought him to school I would either pack him a lunch that he liked, or give him money to buy lunch.

From kindergarten through grade five, the school would allow parents to come have lunch with their kids at school. Jonathan loved having me come to eat lunch with him. I typically came to his school at least once or twice a week to eat lunch with him, and I would bring him something from McDonalds, Wendy's, or Burger King. We kept the fast food industry in business!

Actually, I just wanted Jonathan to have some security in his young life. I wanted him to know he could always count on me, and that I loved him unconditionally. Sometimes I would bring a pizza for him and his friends to enjoy. It was such a blessing to see Jonathan and his friends going wild over the pizza surprise! Other times I would cook at home and bring him a fresh home cooked meal. Sometimes my mom or dad would come with me to visit him. Occasionally my sister, or one of his cousins would come too. Because of those occasions, Jonathan knew he had extended family that would also look out for him. Those were great, happy memories.

Now getting back to our mediation, as I mentioned earlier, she had presented to me a proposal to surrender all her parental rights and responsibilities. It didn't surprise me that she wanted to avoid any future responsibility for our son. Not that I wanted or needed any financial assistance from Tiffany over the next several years of Jonathan's life, but just the fact that she couldn't for once in her life step up and be a real parent is truly sickening. What will this fact look like to my son when he is old enough to truly understand that not only was his biological mother violent and abusive, but she was also willing to visibly illustrate her lack of love for anyone other than herself by choosing not to be a part of his life?

Now, I finally had options. I could choose to decline the offer, and move towards a proposal that would have allowed her supervised visitation, once or twice a month, with full custody and parenting time with me, and require that she begin paying child support of at least fifteen hundred dollars a month until he reached the age of eighteen. This option would have allowed her access to Jonathan's life, at least in a small and safe way initially, and could have left the door open for my son's relationship with her to potentially heal. Jonathan certainly didn't want that, as he made it clear that he will never see her again.

Of course, I knew I would need to respect my son's wishes. I understood that there was a significant reason that he felt this way. While I would have preferred him to have some minimal amount of contact with his mom, I had to accept the fact that the relationship with his mother had been destroyed by her, and there was no fixing it. Whatever Tiffany did to him on that last day he was with her must have been horrific. He still hasn't spoken of that day in detail, and possibly never will. I had to accept that I could not fix this, and that hopefully, in his own time, and in his own way, someday he will be able to come to a place in his life where he can forgive her for all she's done. I pray that day comes, because I know that it will be a part of his healing process, and will bring him closer to God.

After realizing I could never force her to be a mother, and I could never force her to love him the way a parent should, it would be best to proceed with an agreement that would include the termination of her parental rights.

We had faced some difficulties in regards to all the financial details. Tiffany and her attorney placed a bunch of little provisions in the agreement, mostly to protect her from any future financial responsibility. All of that was fine with me, but I was stuck on the return of the money that was owed to me. My attorney was scared that if I continued to hold out for the money that was owed to me, it could sabotage the whole deal. He was very much opposed to me holding out for what was due to me.

As Mr. Anderson and I were going back and forth about the financial details of the agreement, he said to me, "John, when I left my office this morning, I told my wife (Legal Assistant), that this isn't going to happen, there's no way, it's impossible." I responded, "With all due respect Mr. Anderson, I hired you because you are the very best at what you do, but you simply do not know what I know." He said "John, I have to rely on my experience, not on your omniscience." After this, we continued to debate the issue of finances until we ended up having to take a break because her attorney had another hearing in a courtroom down the hall with another client.

We took a break for about thirty minutes. I remember my attorney walking up to me in the hallway. We discussed the direction that this was going, and he was very concerned that the thirty-minute break would give her time to think about what she was about to agree to and would make her change her mind and leave. I admit, that as the time continued to pass, I realized that there was a realistic possibility of that happening. But in my soul, I knew that all was well. I told him again, that there is no way possible that she could leave this building without putting ink to paper. I think he had mistaken my confidence for foolishness. I can't blame him. If I were him, I would have thought the same thing. As Mr. Anderson left to take a break, my mom and I sat down on the bench. Tiffany and her husband remained in their conference room while I answered my mom's questions about the case. I had explained to her where we had arrived at in our negotiations, how much further we had to go, and my attorneys concerns about us trying to go the full distance. My mom also expressed concern that Tiffany could walk away. I told her, "Let's look at all that we have to work with here. If she were to walk away today, God will not have mercy on her. It is His will that my son come home, and there is nothing she can do to stop it. All the forces of darkness cannot stop what God has promised."

I was literally standing face to face with the prince of darkness, and she had no power over me. If Tiffany didn't sign, what would she have to look forward to? Even from just a logical perspective, it didn't make sense to walk away. Tiffany knew she would be facing another deposition, with more and more crimes being exposed. Then her husband, and mother -in - law will be deposed, again exposing numerous crimes. If she were to walk away, the next time she walked into a family courtroom, she would be wearing an orange jumpsuit and shiny silver bracelets around her wrists. I then told my mother, "If her and her husband want to rot away in prison for the next several years, that is their choice. It would not be me that caused that fate to come upon them. They would be walking into it all on their own." Then I tried to explain the situation to her in a spiritual sense. "You remember the story of Moses, right? In the Bible, the story of Moses leading the Israelites out of slavery had described Pharaoh's resistance to God's will. When Moses went to the most powerful man in the nation, and commanded him to free the Israelites, he wasn't walking into that place on his own strength and power. If Moses did not have God standing with him, he surely would've fallen. He would've been a fool to stand in front of Pharaoh with such outrageous demands. Moses brought God's command to Pharaoh repeatedly, and each time Pharaoh refused. Every time he refused, God unleashed a plague against his nation. It wasn't until the plague had taken Pharaoh's son, and all the nation's first-born children, that Pharaoh finally surrendered. If Tiffany walks out of these doors without surrendering to God's will, God will open up the floodgates of heaven and His wrath will come crashing down upon her. It will be beyond horrific." Those were the words I had said. And considering the fact that the papers hadn't been finalized or signed yet, I was certainly taking an enormous leap of faith in speaking such faith filled words. Had I been wrong, it would've made me look insane. I can see how at that moment it could have appeared to be that way to Mr. Anderson. But there was no reason to worry. Because I was not wrong. It was God I was counting on, not myself!

A little while later, the attorneys returned, and we went back to our separate meeting rooms. We went back and forth for a while, but we eventually arrived at a deal that would allow for the termination of her parental rights and responsibilities, as well as the reimbursement of the child support payments I made to her over the past four and a half months, and a very modest payment of $400 a month from her for the past four and a half months from her for our son's support. The only thing Tiffany didn't agree to was the reimbursement of legal fees. My attorney and I discussed this, and while she illegally initiated the litigation, causing the legal expense to be unfairly imposed upon me, we had agreed that if she hadn't initiated a lawsuit, that I would've done so at some point in time anyway.

Mr. Anderson and I had talked for several years prior to this round of litigation, and had discussed my intent to modify custody when my son reached an age that he would be strong enough to stand against her. He knew as well as I did, that this was all destined to happen, with or without Tiffany striking first. Realizing that the financial loss was simply one of the casualties of war, we agreed that we could forget about the reimbursement of legal fees and come to an agreement.

We finalized the terms of the agreement, and the documents were printed and brought into our meeting room for signatures. We read through the papers one last time before signing. Mr. Anderson had the pen in his hand, just about to sign the documents. He sat there for several moments with the most bewildered look on his face. His eyes looked like they had seen a ghost. He appeared to be in shock. Then after a few moments of silence, he said, "I don't believe it." He then signed the papers, and handed them to me for my signatures.

Mr. Anderson couldn't believe what he had just witnessed. He couldn't believe that the impossible had just happened. I could see by the incredulous look on his face that he was having a shock wave of emotions hitting him. He had such a difficult time reconciling in his mind all that had just taken place.

We then walked over to the clerk's office to have the papers notarized, and then filed with the clerk of the courts office so they could be sent to the judge for signing. Jonathan was at school that day, during the mediation. He was of course very anxious to find out what his future held. He had also asked me to tell my attorney to ask her to bring his belongings that he had at her house. Tiffany didn't of course. I texted Jonathan while he was still at school, and told him "It is finished, we won!"

Later when I picked him up from school he asked about his stuff, and I had to tell him that she didn't give it back to us, so he was upset about that.

After the mediation was finished, I invited Mr. Anderson to have lunch with us, but he said he had to go back to his office to work. My mom, dad and I had left the parking lot, and began heading towards Sonny's BBQ for lunch. My wife had been working overnight the night before and had just come home from work that morning. She met us at Sonny's for lunch. I remember that as we were driving, my mom had begun to express her joy for what had just been accomplished, but then she also expressed her hunger for justice.

My mom said, "That witch will pay for all that she has done. She's going to burn in hell." When I heard this, my soul was saddened. You see, as it says in 2 Peter 3:9, that it is not His will for anyone to perish, but that everyone should repent. I told my mom this. I reminded her that at the very last moment of his life, the sinner hanging on the cross next to Jesus had expressed his heart of repentance and Jesus forgave him.

I told my mom that if Tiffany were to die today, without knowing God, she would indeed spend her eternity in hell. But that if someday she repented and gave her life to God, even after all the horrible things that she's done, it would be possible for her to be forgiven and spend her eternity in heaven. I told my mom that God's will is what our will should be, and that we should pray for her healing and salvation.

Chapter Thirty-Eight
The Chains Are Broken

I'll tell you, this was an unfamiliar, but wonderful feeling. It felt like I was dreaming, but I knew I wasn't. For years I lived like I was in prison. Now and then I'd go before the judge pleading for mine and my son's release. The judge would ask, "How do you plead?" My son and I would say, "We plead not guilty. We are innocent!" Each time the gavel came down, with a resounding, "NO, you will not go free." In fact, each time we went to court, we were sentenced to serve more hard time.

Then, in an instant, I'm released from prison, after being falsely accused and serving fourteen years of hard time for something I didn't do. It was my first moment of freedom, and my first moment of life without the chains that have held me down for so long. I had my whole life ahead of me. I could go where ever I wanted to go, and do what ever I wanted to do.

Most of all, I was free to love my son and wife without having to look over my shoulders, wondering when the next storm would be coming.

I could raise my son without fear. Terror no longer held me in its grip. Fear could not control me. I'm now able to live my life without wondering when the next false accusation will come. I can live my life without wondering if I will be put behind bars for something I didn't do. I can live my life knowing that my son is also free. He will not ever be held by the chains of fear. Jonathan won't know what it is like to live the rest of his life hounded by an abusive and enraged mother. Fear is no longer the beast that controls him. Fear is defeated and destroyed. What an exhilarating feeling! Everything that was old has passed away, and everything is now new. It was a feeling like no other. It was like being born again.

When we arrived at the restaurant, my mom, my dad, my wife and I all sat at the table, and after we ordered our food, the strangest thing happened. Tiffany and her husband walked in and sat down at a table. I'm sure it was just a coincidence that they happened to choose the same place as us for lunch, but then again, with all the stalking she has done throughout the years, I wouldn't be surprised if she had followed us there, or had her husband make a call to a buddy of his at the sheriff's office to find the GPS coordinates of my phone in order to follow us to our destination.

While I am kind of kidding, I'm kind of not kidding. Either way, it doesn't matter. I know Tiffany had her husband abuse the power of the sheriff's office many times. But it was of no concern to me what she was doing, even if it did violate my rights. Why would I care? I was free. She couldn't touch me. Tiffany would have to go through the Almighty God to get to me or my son. And that's something she could never do.

As we sat there waiting for our food, I went through my Facebook posts from years ago, to find something that I posted in late 2014. It was then, back in November 2014 that God had told me: "I will move the heavens and the earth to make a way for him." He had promised me this, and when He did, I had proudly posted it on Facebook for all to see. I showed my mom, dad and wife, the post I made on November 7th, 2014, where I quoted God on His promise. As John 14:29 states, "I have told you these things before they happen, so that when they do happen, that you will believe that I Am Who I Am". I knew that by sharing His promise with others many years before it was to be fulfilled, that when it was fulfilled, they would know that it was God that had done it. There could be no denying this truth. I alone could not have known that the impossible would someday become possible. Only He could promise such a miracle, and only He could accomplish the impossible. There was not one tongue that could utter a word against this truth. God had worked this miracle in our lives. It was just moments later that I felt compelled to tell my family that I was going to write a book. I had made the decision many years earlier. Long before the final chapters of the story that God had already written, had played out.

I even tried once, several years earlier, to get a head start on the book, but after just a few pages, I realized that I couldn't find the words to write, that I didn't know how to tell the story. I suppose it simply wasn't the right time back then. I abandoned the thought of writing it. It wasn't until November 14th, 2016, just weeks after God had physically brought my son home, but many months before it was finalized, that I began to write again, and wrote only the first paragraph of this book. I would not end up writing any more than that first paragraph until May 2017. And here I am, it's April 26, 2018, almost a year after starting the first chapter, that I am writing this final chapter.

Chapter Thirty-Nine

The Truth Has Set Us Free

I want to share my final thoughts on all that has happened. I feel like Job from the Bible. God allowed Satan to push Job all the way to the edge. Satan had taken away Job's wealth, his health, and his family. All the while, Job refused to turn away from God. During the most difficult times in his life, when he should've surrendered to the circumstances, he chose to surrender only to God. At one point, his wife even told him to curse God and die. He endured all these difficulties, trusting that God would always be there for him. God had allowed Satan to push him to the limit, but would never allow Satan to push him beyond the limit's that He had set forth.

Satan was certain that he could break Job. He was sure he could make Job turn against God. In the end, not only did Job not turn against God, but in the end, after Job had endured these tests, God restored all that had been taken from him, and more. In the end, it was the enemy that surrendered. The reason Satan surrendered in the end was because Job had surrendered to God in the beginning. I chose to surrender to God in the beginning, and because of that, Tiffany surrendered in the end.

While his mother had always caused heartache and destruction, I still must remember to appreciate the good times my son and I had throughout the years. And now, even though we are in the middle of the teenage years, we are still having some of the best times of our lives. He has grown so much. He is no longer that scared and timid young boy that used to have to endure all the abuse that comes from living with a parent that has borderline personality disorder.

He is now a healthy, strong, and much happier young man. Free from the chains that have enslaved him for so many of his years on this earth. I too have had those same chains broken. I am now free from living in fear, free from the threats of violence, false imprisonment, and free from the past threats and attempts on my life. While we still currently live in the same community that we lived in since his birth, and are still only miles away from his mother. Thus far, since the court case has been finalized, she has no longer continued to invade our lives with pain and destruction.

I would love to move far away from the battle site, but he enjoys living near all of his friends. Taking my son away from all of them and bringing him to another place where he knows no one would be difficult for him right now. Considering that he is just barely beginning the healing process, and presumably has many years of healing ahead of him, I don't want to further disrupt his life.

While my family and I will always be aware of the possibility of the threat reemerging, we now have chosen to trust in God for our peace and for our safety. Tiffany no longer holds the threat of hurting my son or falsely imprisoning me over my head in order to control and manipulate our lives for her own entertainment and pleasure. If she ever wishes to try to take my life again, she can do so. If she believes that she has the authority to determine when my life ends, she is sadly mistaken. God is in control. I may not have realized it many years ago, but He always has been, and He always will be in control.

For the time being, we will remain where we are, happy and free. And after all, I still have my home, my business, and now my wife and her family and mine here in Florida. I told my mom fifteen years ago when she told me to run, that there is no man, women, child or beast on the face of God's green earth that could ever tear down this house, because this is the house that God built. I can show you that the promise was true by the fact that everything that God has built in my life is still standing.

After fifteen years, and after many, many attempts to destroy my life, I'm still standing. Tiffany is the one, through no effort of mine, who has stumbled and fallen. She is the one that has fallen over her own choices, and her own attempts to destroy me. Throughout all of these years and throughout all the attacks, I can proudly confess that not once have I ever responded with an attack. Never did I bear false witness against her. I never attempted to harm her. Nor did I ever attempt to repay evil with evil. Not once. I knew from the beginning, if I were to ever enjoy the moment where I see God's promise fulfilled, I would have to always walk in His light, and I would always have to walk in His ways. I had enough wisdom early on to surrender it all to Him, and patiently, and painfully, wait for Him and His perfect will for our lives, and His perfect timing.

Living under the promise of God has truly been an exhilarating experience. It reminds me of His Word, where He says in Mark 16:18, "They will pick up snakes with their hands, and they will drink deadly poison, and it will not hurt them at all, and they will lay their hands -on sick people, and they will get well". This is the power that lives within the Word of God, and within those that have the Word living in them. I had been forced to endure Tiffany's constant attacks throughout the years, and had no choice but to humble myself each time, giving her everything she demanded. Money, power, and control was surrendered to her for so many years. It was all I could do to satisfy her hunger and thirst for destruction.

It was all I could do to shield my son the best that I could from the wrath of the beast. I had to constantly surrender, knowing all the while that my son was suffering. I surrendered, so that his suffering wouldn't be increased. He would tell me many times throughout the years, even as a young child, to just give his mom whatever she wanted to try to keep her calm, so that he wouldn't have to endure the wrath of an angry beast. It was difficult enough for him to endure the wrath of the beast without making it even harder by making the beast angry.

Tiffany must have thought she had me under her control, and that I had surrendered to her. Tiffany had no idea that with the promise of God living inside of my heart, that it was not her I was surrendering to, but it was God that I was surrendering to. She didn't realize that God was in control all along. You see, every time my boy came home with burns, bruises, and fear in his heart, I would ask God, "Why not now God?" He would answer, "Not yet". I did not understand why He was delaying His promise. Even to this day I'm not sure if I understand.

The only theory I have, and even my son, now 15 years old had theorized, is that maybe we went through everything we did in order to have this story to tell. It's now April of 2018, and I was at the mall in Orlando with my son Jonathan and his friend having lunch, when I told him that this story is going to be made into a book. He said, "Maybe that's why all of this happened, so that you can become a famous author".

I thought it was interesting that he was able to understand that sometimes something bad must happen in order for something good to come from it. He was able to see that tragedies can sometimes lead to triumph. Being a child, he sees the triumph as the possibility of his dad becoming a famous author. The real triumph is being able to tell the world about what God has done in our lives. The real triumph is God being glorified through the story of our trials and our victories. The real triumph is sharing our story of suffering, and the **faith** that we had during those tough times.

The real triumph is sharing our story of **love**. Love that would lead a man to risk his life and his freedom, and sacrifice his peace and safety, all for the love of his son. The real triumph is to share our story of how, after all that we had been through, just like Jesus did on the cross, when He prayed to God to forgive those who were murdering Him, that we too can have **forgiveness** in our hearts for those that have persecuted us. The real triumph is to be able to replicate the nature and character of our God by choosing to live with the same love in our hearts for others, and the heart of forgiveness that God Himself has. These are the real triumphs that we have experienced as a result of our tragedies.

Now that all is said and done, the last words that I would like to share with Tiffany, is, "Thank you". Thank you for giving me the greatest gifts that anyone has ever given me. The gift of my son, and the gift of this story. The Name (God) that you have cursed for so many years, is the same Name that you have glorified through the sharing of this testimony. And in the end, all there is left for me to do, is to leave you with these last words, "I forgive you".

49959828R00171

Made in the USA
Columbia, SC
30 January 2019